IMAGES
of England

HILLINGDON
CINEMAS

A July 1913 poster for the Empire Electric – Uxbridge's second cinema.

IMAGES
of England

HILLINGDON
CINEMAS

James Skinner

TEMPUS

First published 2002
Copyright © James Skinner, 2002

Tempus Publishing Limited
The Mill, Brimscombe Port,
Stroud, Gloucestershire, GL5 2QG

ISBN 0 7524 2610 9

Typesetting and origination by
Tempus Publishing Limited
Printed in Great Britain by
Midway Colour Print, Wiltshire

Dedication

This book is dedicated to my wife Joy who, for many years, has listened patiently to my nostalgic reminiscences about the old picture palaces and accompanied me regularly to those dens of delight.

Contents

Acknowledgements

I am sincerely grateful to the following for their help in the researching of this book, and also for the loan of personal photographs and other material:

Ken Pearce, Don Mead, Carolynne Cotton, Gwyn Jones, Eric Bond Hutton, Lewis Glassman, Doreen Bromfield, Barbara Hill, Ralph Rumble, Chris Wren, Adela Harrison, Tim Leman, Gloria Mullaney, Vera Baker, Gordon Ogbourne, Douglas Rust, Audrey Skinner, Tim Ripley (Odeon Cinemas).

My thanks are also due to the Heritage Department of Uxbridge Central Library and the borough's history societies for allowing me access to their records; to the Cinema Theatre Association; Gazette Newspapers (formerly *Middlesex Advertiser and Gazette*); Taylor Woodrow PLC; Philip Sherwood; Tony Thrasher; Chris Clegg; and M. Frances Brum for permission to reproduce their photographs.

Finally, a special thank you to Charlotte Skinner for processing my manuscript.

Introduction

This is a story of successes and failures; of highs and lows; and the rapid rise and dramatic decline of our cinemas. The story is not unique, for although it is about Hillingdon and West Middlesex, readers undoubtedly will identify with a scenario that could apply to any average-sized town in the UK.

It is the story of how the public's imagination was captured by flickering shadows on a silver screen – from the time of so-called 'penny gaffs' at the beginning of the twentieth century, progressing to the more salubriously titled 'electric theatres', and finally to the halcyon days of the 'dream palaces', created in the 1930s.

When it superseded the magic lantern, the advent of the cinematograph drew excited crowds like moths to a flame, as they flocked to see the spectacle of images that actually moved. But the excitement mounted to fever pitch with the coming of sound in 1928/29. The 'talkies' had arrived, and people were immediately hooked on what would soon become the nation's – if not the world's – premier form of entertainment for the next three decades at least, though there were those who predicted that the new medium would never catch on!

The boom began in the early thirties, in the social climate spawned by the Depression. New cinemas sprang up like mushrooms and picture-going provided an escape route where people could forget their troubles for a few hours. By 1934, admissions in Britain totalled 957 million, and in November that year, film distributors warned that there was an excess of cinemas, and that many of them would have to close. They could not have been more wrong, as two years later press reports revealed that cinema-goers were spending £40 million a year on 950 million tickets at an average price of less than one shilling. At the outbreak of war in 1939 there were 5,500 cinemas nationwide. Throughout the 1940s attendances soared to even higher levels, and it was recorded that in one week in January 1940 at the Odeon flagship cinema in Leicester Square, 27,702 people paid to see *The Stars Look Down*, despite the Blitz, blackout and icy weather.

While on the subject of statistics, my personal cinema activities reached an all-time high during 1941 and 1942, when I saw a total of 650 films at our local cinemas. The figure includes second features, but still averages out at three visits a week which, in the middle of the Second World War, was not at all uncommon.

But the next decade, the 1950s, saw the start of the decline not only of our Hillingdon cinemas but of cinemas throughout the country. Television was almost certainly the main contributory factor, and between 1950 and 1956 attendances dropped dramatically. Over the next three years, the Rank company alone closed ninety-one of their houses, with another fifty-seven earmarked for the same fate – it could be termed the fall of the Rank empire. So the downward spiral continued and by 1980, eighty per cent of all cinemas had been lost.

However, one final statistic offers a ray of hope for the future. Records show that there were 142 million admissions in the UK during 2000, which represented an increase of sixty per cent over the previous ten years. Predictions indicate that this resurgence will continue.

It is nearly fifty years since the bulldozers first moved in to wreak their own particular kind of vandalism on our borough's and the nation's cinemas, thus depriving the younger and future generations of the opportunity to see these picture palaces in the flesh. This makes the work of English Heritage the more commendable as they endeavour to list, preserve and upgrade the few that are still standing. And, somewhat perversely, the old enemy – television – has partly atoned for the role it played in bringing down these buildings by providing us with means of viewing the old films again – not in palatial splendour, but nevertheless in the comfort of our own 'armchair Odeon'!

Some cinema historians have admitted to being more interested in admiring the auditorium décor than what was happening on the screen. For me, it was the reverse. But like so many aspects of life that are no longer with us, the 'dream palaces' are now more fully appreciated and fondly remembered than ever before, by me and, I suspect, by many others besides.

I trust that this story will rekindle some nostalgic memories for those who experienced the events as they occurred and, for those who are too young to remember, I hope I have been able to conjure up a mental picture of the way things were, way back when.

One

Uxbridge:From Penny Gaff to Multiplex

Shackleton had just completed his historical expedition to the South Pole; Blériot his record breaking flight across the Channel in 43 minutes; Selfridges opened in Oxford Street; Manchester United won the FA Cup and Mary Pickford was dubbed 'The World's Sweetheart'. It was 1909 and in the Surrey country town of Guildford, a twenty-six-year-old man was attending a trade exhibition at the town hall. His name was John Percy William Hutton.

A strong spirit of adventure had already led Jack (as he was always known) to South Africa where he spent some years developing a successful business. But after contracting a fever, he returned home to England. Unable to settle down, the wanderlust took over, and he sailed for America. There, he became fascinated by the cinema business, which was becoming well established in the States, although still in its infancy in Britain. After a few months he came back full of ideas for the promotion of moving pictures, and during his visit to the Guildford exhibition, he was advised by the organizer that Uxbridge could be a likely venue for such a venture. His immediate response was, 'Where's Uxbridge?'

Obviously, for a globetrotter like Jack, the town did not take much finding, and after travelling there by tram from Shepherd's Bush, he spent a day walking around looking for a prospective site. He found a suitable hall – St Margaret's in Belmont Road – but was told that it was definitely not available. However, a fortnight later, he was notified that a building known as Rockingham Hall in The Lynch, which had stood empty for a long time, might be suitable. Mr Hutton agreed, and so began his new career as a show business entrepreneur. There had been magic lantern and even kinematograph shows in Uxbridge, in particular at the Theatre Royal in Chapel Street, but Jack Hutton, once described by the press as 'the man who made Uxbridge', must receive full credit for introducing the first purpose-built cinema to the town. Indeed, it was the first in the whole of the district that would eventually make up the borough of Hillingdon.

Jack's first task was to thoroughly overhaul and renovate the building to ensure that it complied with the regulations laid down by the Cinematograph Act of 1909, which became operative on 1 January 1910. The Middlesex County Council Licensing Committee met on 6 January to implement the new act and grant licences accordingly. It was reported that during the first year, a total of forty-four licences was issued throughout the county, but anyone would be hard pressed to locate this number of Middlesex cinemas in 1910!

Jack Hutton's promise to his prospective patrons was 'to provide first-class films' and the management's policy was 'to give full value for popular prices'. These were 3d and 6d for the twice-nightly performances at 7 p.m. and 9 p.m., while the children's price for the two Saturday afternoon matinées was 1d. A pianist provided the musical accompaniment to the 'silents'; the projector was hand operated and the programme changed every Monday and Thursday. The opening performance took place on Saturday 6 August 1910, the event being recorded in the 11 August issue of the trade journal *Kinematograph and Lantern Weekly*. Although the Rockingham Hall had a seating capacity of 256, and screened fourteen performances every week, it soon became apparent that it could not cope with the demands of large crowds who flocked to see the new entertainment medium. As a result, only two months later, a local photographer, Mr Billinghurst, opened a second cinema just a short distance away in Vine Street. Known initially as the Empire Hall, it had been built on the same site where circus-type entertainment had taken place in a large tent during the previous century. And it was decidedly 'upmarket' compared with the old Rockingham Hall.

It opened on Wednesday 5 October, and the next day's issue of the *Kinematograph and Lantern Weekly* included a detailed description as follows:

'On Wednesday, the Empire Hall was comfortably filled for the first show of pictures. Passing up the steps, one entered by a curtained doorway, and at once obtained a view of the screen. The programme opened at 6.45 p.m. The building is brick-built, with slated roof supported by iron girders, and the floor, which is sloped from back to front, gives each and all the same opportunity of seeing. The screen is 15ft by 12ft in measurement. The seating accommodates 400. The 3d seats have 3 inches more knee-room than the regulations require, while even more space is given in the 6d rows. Down each side of the hall (which measured 74ft by 40ft) is a 4ft gangway, while the two exit doors are connected by another wide gangway, crossing the room at right angles. Besides these, there are two emergency exits and one other ordinary exit, all the doors being opened from the inside on the push-bar principle. The screen on which the pictures are shown is of a special character, being of Portland cement, faced with a finer cement, and finally treated with Hall's distemper, giving a perfectly smooth dead-white and rigid ground for the pictures.'

The last sentence of the report appears to be a good advert for the two firms mentioned!

From the outset there was fierce competition between the two rival managers, each trying to outdo the other with a series of innovations and gimmicks, and it appeared to be a case of 'anything you can do, I can do better'. Jack Hutton had a stage erected in his Rockingham Hall for variety acts, which he promised at every performance in addition to the films, and staged competitions in singing, dancing, reciting, and what was listed as 'patter' – presumably stand-up comedy. The winners would receive excellent prizes, including a week's engagement at the theatre.

The Empire retaliated with a beauty contest for young ladies – then one for babies up to three years old, and children up to twelve. 'Bring photographs to the pay box,' the advertisements read, and went on: 'The selected twelve will be shown on the screen, and the audience will decide by voting to whom the prizes shall be given.' In the case of the ladies, these were two gold watches, with unnamed equivalents for the babies. Another innovation introduced by the Empire manager was the installation of radiators to ensure 'the Hall will be kept comfortably warmed for the winter months'.

Mr Hutton's advertisements during these early encounters were somewhat provocative, with headlines like 'We were the first'; 'We lead – others follow'; and 'There are pictures and pictures, but our pictures are the best'. He also proclaimed 'our coloured pictures a speciality', although what these consisted of in 1910 is not clear. The Empire's reaction to this was to bring in a concession whereby 150 of the 3d seats were reduced to 2d until 8 p.m., every night except Saturdays.

However, after only a year, and rather surprisingly, the Empire had not proved entirely successful. Perhaps it was an omen when on opening night the picture was, allegedly, shown upside down! But whatever the reason, the enterprising Jack Hutton now saw his opportunity to move upmarket. He formed a limited company, and in September 1911 acquired the cinema, which, by then, had assumed the much grander title of the 'Empire Electric Theatre'. After a week spent effecting repairs and renovation to ensure 'that it will be in thorough working order for a first-class winter session', Mr Hutton reopened his new acquisition on 16 September 1911.

Bringing with him a combination of showmanship and business expertise, he achieved almost instant success. He rented the masterpieces of the day – *Quo Vadis*,

A wartime picture of what was originally the Theatre Royal in Chapel Street, Uxbridge – venue of the first kinematograph shows in the town.

A local newspaper advertisement for the opening of Uxbridge's first cinema, in 1910.

Les Misérables, *The Miracle*, *Dr Jekyll and Mr Hyde*, and *Ivanhoe*, in addition to *Lady Audley's Secret* and *The Cowboy Millionaire*. When *Quo Vadis* was playing, the press reported 'it was difficult for pedestrians to thread their way along Vine Street, while inside the theatre, patrons were thankful to have standing accommodation'. Jack produced a six-page programme of events, with his picture and one of the cinema on the front cover, and also introduced a children's matinée on Saturday afternoons when admission was 1d or 2d, with the youngsters being given sweets or oranges as a bonus.

In addition to the films, he regularly staged a number of variety and charity concerts, and occasionally he filled in by singing a song or two in the interval. A piano or organ, and sometimes both, always accompanied the silent pictures. The local press frequently commented on his undoubted popularity as the general manager, as he continued to give the public what it wanted, and by April 1913, with the Empire now a thriving concern, he advertised that his first cinema, Rockingham Hall, was to let. Eventually, it was purchased by the Twinn family for use as a corn store, and they still own the property, now converted into offices.

At the outbreak of the First World War in 1914, Jack was in negotiations for the purchase of a cinema in nearby Southall, but that plan was dropped when he enlisted in the 8th Middlesex Regiment. Jack's daughter, Adela Harrison, now a sprightly eighty-nine-year-old who prefers to be known as Addie, told me her father had 'gone off to war, leaving her mother Ada and his business partner to manage the cinema'. Addie confirmed that her mother continued to man the pay box (as she had done from the outset) until the day she decided she wanted a change from the picture business and bought a fish shop in Windsor Street. Jack was still serving abroad in France, Egypt and Gibraltar, and Addie recalled how she and her mother lived in a flat above the shop until her father's discharge in 1919.

It was then Jack's turn to change direction, and devoting all his energies and bringing his business acumen to the new venture, he built up a chain of fish shops throughout the borough which totalled thirty-three by the time he died in 1960. And when he disposed of the Empire to a new owner, although it was advertised as being 'Under entirely new management', his name was not far away, for immediately above the cinema advertisement was a block the same size reading 'Jack Hutton's Fish and Chip Shop'. Truly, he was a real entrepreneur.

Hardly surprisingly, his daughter Addie summed up Jack Hutton's career and love affair with the town as follows: 'He was an astute businessman who did an awful lot for Uxbridge,' obviously referring to his countless involvements with the community, quite apart from introducing the silver screen.

Whether by luck or judgement, it soon transpired that the Huttons' decision to quit the Empire was the right one, for them anyway, as shortly afterwards, in 1921, the infinitely superior Savoy was built at the top of the same street. However, the old cinema continued to operate and endeavoured to compete for a few more years. In 1923, the new owners had instigated what their advertisements described as a 'good orchestra' instead of the solo piano or organ, and on Sundays they hired out the building for religious meetings. The ownership passed to a London company in 1927, but the Empire ceased to operate after only two years. Then, after remaining empty until 1932, it was purchased by Uxbridge Urban District Council, which converted it into a fire station by March 1933.

A group of Uxbridge's first cinema-goers outside Rockingham Hall, in 1910. The owner Mr Hutton is the gentleman in the boater on the left of the picture.

John (Jack) Hutton, who introduced the cinema to Uxbridge. This portrait was taken in the photographic studio of Mr W.G. Taylor – whose premises were immediately opposite the Empire Electric Theatre in Vine Street.

A recent picture of Jack Hutton's daughter, Mrs Adela Harrison, photographed outside her father's first cinema, Rockingham Hall, now converted into offices.

Rockingham Hall in The Lynch, as it is today.

A local press announcement of the opening of the Empire Hall in Vine Street in 1910. Later, it would be known as the Empire Electric.

EMPIRE HALL
PICTURE PALACE
Vine Street, UXBRIDGE.
(OPPOSITE RAILWAY STATION.)

Just a Reminder !

Next Week keep at least one evening free to visit the above, when an Interesting, Laughable, Instructive, and High - Class Entertainment of the best and latest Living Pictures will be shown.

Open Every Evening at 6.45
Wednesdays & Saturdays at 3.15 p.m.

COME IN WHEN YOU LIKE.
NO WAITING.
Every person can occupy a separate, comfortable, tip-up seat, as fixed in all the leading places of amusement in London.

CONTINUOUS PROGRAMME
— From 6.45 p.m. —

Complete Change of Pictures
Twice Weekly.

Admission 3d. Reserved Seats 6d.

Advertisements for the two rival cinemas juxtaposed in a November 1910 newspaper.

A 1913 programme cover for the Empire Electric.

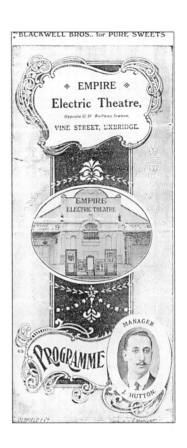

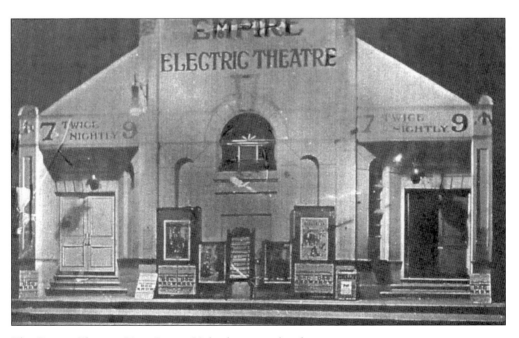

The Empire Electric, Vine Street, Uxbridge, in its heyday.

The Empire Electric in 1932, displaying 'sold' notices on its doors instead of cinema posters, shortly before its conversion to a fire station.

Before the coming of the Empire's main competitor, the Savoy, another cinema had appeared on the local scene at an unlikely venue – the RAF station at the eastern end of the High Street. In no way did it try to compete with the town's existing or even future cinemas, but it was nevertheless a welcome addition to the residents' entertainment.

Built just before the end of the First World War in 1918, it replaced a small hut-like cinema near the Vine Lane entrance at the Hillingdon end of the camp. The new building was sited just inside the camp boundary adjacent to the main Hillingdon road, and almost opposite St Andrew's church. Originally designed as a general-purpose lecture hall for instructing new cadets of the newly named Royal Air Force, which before 1 April 1918 was known as the Royal Flying Corps, it was a plain brick and slate building without any frills or fancy décor. There was no balcony, no luxury carpeting, and the seating was very basic on a non-sloping floor – although double seats in the back rows were a notable feature. But it did include a good-sized stage, dressing rooms and a projection box.

The opening night, Thursday 2 May 1919, took the form of a big variety concert including singers and other artistes, accompanied by a full orchestra. A Charlie Chaplin picture and another short film completed the programme. In the hall's early days it appeared that the RAF was content to limit the use of the building to lectures and stage productions by local musical societies. In 1921, the Uxbridge Operatic Society performed *The Mikado* and *Faust*, and when these shows were advertised in the local press, the venue was described as 'RAF Lecture Hall'. Two years later, it became 'RAF Lecture Hall (Cinema)' and finally 'RAF Cinema'. But despite the new title in the press advertisements, live concerts were still being staged regularly and the Metropolitan Police Minstrel Show was an annual event. No films were advertised until the mid-twenties, probably because originally the general public had not been admitted to these unless accompanied by service personnel. But when the rule was relaxed, the hall became a full-time picture house.

In 1922, a new RAF recruit calling himself Aircraftman John Ross attended lectures in the hall, and wrote about them in his book *The Mint*. His real name was T.E. Lawrence – better known as Lawrence of Arabia.

By 1927, the cinema was operating six days a week, with musical accompaniment for the silent movies provided by local piano teacher, Mrs Mabel Walters. There was a change of programme every Monday and Thursday, although after Sunday opening was legalized in 1933/34, the programmes ran from Sunday to Wednesday and Thursday to Saturday. This arrangement differed from the other houses which all screened a separate Sunday programme for one day only.

The films shown were always second or even third time around, and often much later than their first outings at the other local cinemas. But invariably, most of the programmes consisted of two main features, so were good value for money, especially as the 'Camp' (as it came to be known) offered lower admission prices than elsewhere. One example of this was the children's price of 3d compared with 4d at the Regal and Odeon. And the main point in the cinema's favour was the opportunity it afforded for catching up with films missed on their general release.

As far as one can tell, the 'Camp' rarely, if ever, enjoyed packed houses or patrons

A recent picture of the Camp Cinema at the RAF station, Uxbridge. The building has remained almost unchanged since it was built in 1919.

Another view of the RAF Camp Cinema.

queuing at its doors, but it continued to provide a useful service throughout the thirties until it was obliged to close at the outbreak of the Second World War in September 1939. Unlike the other cinemas, it would never reopen as a picture house, and on Saturday 2 September, it screened its final film – *The Green Light,* starring Errol Flynn. Subsequently the building was converted into a gymnasium, and it was also used for an important event at the beginning of June 1944, when the RAF received its briefing there for the D-Day landings of 6 June. After the war, it was again used as a theatre by RAF drama groups and other local dramatic societies.

Today, the building is exactly as it was when first built in 1918. But inside, sadly, it shows all the signs of deterioration, through lack of use and maintenance. Worst affected are the projection boxes, cloakrooms and backstage area, although the auditorium itself is in reasonable condition. During a recent visit, I gathered that the powers that be are debating whether to apply for listed building status, or to pull it down! As it is one of only four of the borough's twenty-two cinema buildings still standing, dare we hope they do not choose the latter option?

The Savoy was built on the site of the old town hall, or public rooms, by the firm of Mr Albert Boyer, to the design of Mr Williams from the Covent Garden based architects Williams and Cox. A fairly impressive building on the corner of Vine Street and the High Street, its frontage resembled a Georgian town house rather than a cinema. The interior was long and narrow, measuring 140ft by 31ft, and attractively decorated in two delicate shades of heliotrope. Despite its narrow entrance, the foyer was pleasing enough with its eye-catching large black and white floor tiles, two pay boxes and a stairway leading to the circle containing 348 seats. The downstairs auditorium housed 666 seats, set out in three blocks divided by two aisles, and the total capacity was almost three times that of the nearby Empire. The proprietors were

Poster for the RAF Camp Cinema, *c.* 1927-28.

Uxbridge Picture Playhouse Ltd, whose managing director was Major Bowlby.

The official opening took place on Monday 3 October 1921, with the screening of the film *Romance*, starring Doris Keane, who was described in the advertisements as 'the greatest emotional actress on the screen'. A specially invited audience assembled for an afternoon performance, which consisted of a newsreel, a short nature film and the main feature. The opening ceremony was performed by Mrs de Salis, deputizing for her husband who was otherwise engaged. A full symphony orchestra supplied the background music for the film and in addition, a well-known singer of the day, Mlle Jose Purnella, gave (according to a review in the *Middlesex Advertiser*) 'a delightful rendering of "Softly Awakes My Heart" from *Samson and Delilah*, while Miss Keane in her role of a grand opera singer, mimed the words up on the screen'. For the evening performance, the doors were opened to the general public at 5 p.m., and the result was a sell-out. And in keeping with most other cinemas at the time, there was a change of programme every Monday and Thursday. Evidently, there was no shortage of silent movies.

An additional facility offered by the Savoy was a tea-room on the first floor. Known as the 'Grey Rooms', it was also used for dances on some Saturday nights, and in late 1923, the cinema advertised whist drives every Thursday at 8 p.m. with a top prize of 50s. A leisure centre of the twenties! Admission prices were listed as 1s 6d for the whist drives, 2s for dances and 'popular prices' for the cinema. Presumably 'popular' meant

R.A.F. Cinema, Uxbridge

To-night (5.30 p.m.) and Sat. (2.30 p.m.)	•	PAUL ROBESON In SHOW BOAT (U) ROBERT WILCOX In GAMBLING SHIP (A)

SUNDAY, 27th AUGUST   FOR 4 DAYS
FROM 5.30 p.m.

I MET A MURDERER
Starring   (A)
James Mason   Pamela Kellino

THE LONG SHOT
— with —   (U)
Gordon JONES   Marsha HUNT

THURSDAY, AUGUST 31st   FOR 3 DAYS
FROM 5.30 p.m. (SATURDAY 2.30 p.m.)

ERROL FLYNN
— In —   (A)
THE GREEN LIGHT

GEORGE BRENT
— In —   (U)
THE GO-GETTER

Newspaper advertisement for the last programmes shown at the Camp Cinema, before closure on 2 September 1939.

cheap, but the more expensive seats in the balcony area were quoted at 1s 10d and 2s 4d and could be booked in advance from Willis's music shop a few yards away. And in 1932 an inducement to patrons was the provision of free bus services from Ickenham, West Drayton and Iver.

Several refurbishment programmes took place during the 1930s, and in 1934 a new outer system of lighting was employed enabling the name 'Savoy' to stand out boldly within a frame of red neon light, with other strips of red around the façade. In its newspaper advertisements, the cinema now described itself as 'The New Savoy' and soon afterwards the ownership passed to the Union Cinema group, who insisted their name appeared in front of the cinema's own name. But apparently, the Union Group had expanded at too fast a rate, and in October 1937, they themselves were swallowed up by the giant Associated British Cinema circuit. So the Savoy joined the increasing ranks of ABC Cinemas. The days of dancing and whist drives in the Grey Rooms had long since gone by the time of the takeover, and the area was used as a private club known as the Korner House Klub. The name 'Union Cinemas' was removed from under the portico, and the familiar triangular ABC logo appeared in the centre of the façade. Then, in July 1938, a further modernization programme 'costing several thousand pounds' effected a complete refurbishment, comprising new sound equipment, a new screen, larger stage and all-new drapes and decorations.

At the outbreak of war on 3 September 1939, the Savoy, along with all the nation's cinemas, was closed by government order. But for the majority, the shutdown was short-lived, and it was back to 'business as usual' after a fortnight. Evidently, the government soon realized what a morale booster the cinema could be, apart from which they probably foresaw what a powerful propaganda weapon film might prove to be in the wartime years that lay ahead. The public now needed escapism more than ever and attendances soared to record heights. The weekly film magazine *Picturegoer* warned people not to arrive at their local cinema without their gas masks. The message went on, 'If you do, you may be politely told that as much as the management would like you to see the show, the order of the day is: No Gas Mask – No Admission.' There is no evidence to suggest that this unwritten law was ever implemented, and I must admit that I never complied. If my memory serves me correctly, neither did anyone else.

Even after the start of the Blitz, the threat of air raids – very real in 1940 – did not deter audiences from filling the cinemas. And if the sirens sounded during a performance, a message to that effect was projected onto the screen, superimposed over the film, which continued to run. This usually resulted in a collective groan from the audience who made no attempt to leave their seats – they weren't going to miss the rest of the film because of an air raid! And a notable example of this occurred at the Savoy on the night of Thursday 7 November 1940, when a bomb hit the front façade of the cinema during the showing of *Edison The Man*, starring Spencer Tracy. A full house had just enjoyed the supporting feature, *Saps at Sea* with Laurel and Hardy, and according to a report in the *Advertiser and Gazette*, they were 'so absorbed in the story of Thomas Edison, that they took little notice of the explosion'. Fortunately, the bomb, one of ten that fell on Uxbridge that evening, failed to penetrate the second floor and lodged in the roof which bore the brunt of the damage. In the projection box, the fourteen-year-old trainee projectionist, Anthony Stagg, was hit on the head by a piece of metal, but carried on manfully assisting his chief, Mr J. Maloney. Between them they ensured that the film continued without interruption until the end. Mr Maloney's

Newspaper advertisement for the opening programme at the Savoy, Uxbridge, 1921.

main concern was the possible damage caused by the bomb to the battery room. But although no one in the Savoy was injured, the blast from the explosion had serious consequences on the other side of the High Street, directly opposite the cinema. An eighty-two-year-old woman and her son were killed in their upstairs flat, and an RAF serviceman was killed by flying glass while walking along the High Street. Some time after the bombing, and possibly as a result of it, the end gable section of the roof was removed together with the three attic-type front windows, considerably changing the appearance of the frontage.

During the forties and fifties, despite being somewhat overshadowed by the town's larger cinemas (the Odeon and the Regal), the Savoy soldiered on and continued to do good business, if the long queues down Vine Street were anything to go by. I regarded that side of the cinema as a sort of 'hellfire' corner, having stood there patiently in the face of howling northerly gales and driving rain during the winter months. To reach the head of the queue, turn the corner and be admitted into the cosy vestibule was a blessed relief. In those days of full houses and continuous performances, it was the job of the usherettes to count the seats vacated by outgoing patrons, and pass the information out to the commissionaire or doorman. So those in the queue eagerly awaited his every appearance, but usually he could allow only a few people in at a time. One man who remembers performing this task is Ruislip resident Gordon Ogbourne, who joined the Savoy staff at the age of fifteen, in 1945. Employed as a pageboy, he, like the main doorman, sported a smart green uniform trimmed with gold braid and a peaked cap. Gordon told me that his other duties included spraying the auditorium with perfume to eliminate the smell of cigarette smoke, collecting fish and chips for

Doris Keane, star of *Romance*, the opening film at the Savoy, Uxbridge.

An example of prominent billboard advertising in the early 1920s.

the manager's dinner, and running between the Savoy and Regal two or three times a day with a copy of the newsreel which both cinemas shared. Eventually, Gordon left to become a trainee projectionist at the Playhouse, Gerrards Cross, and subsequently he achieved his ambition to become chief projectionist at the Beaconsfield Picture House.

As a result of falling attendances throughout the late fifties, the Savoy was the first of the remaining Uxbridge cinemas to close. The British comedies *Doctor at Large* and *Man of the Moment* were the last films to be screened there on Saturday 10 June 1960. An error on the main billboard advertised the main feature as *Doctor in the House*. Perhaps the management was past caring by then! Even their newspaper advertisements were much reduced in size, and on the final one, under the titles, the following announcement appeared:

'**Notice of Closure.** After the performance on Sat. June 10th next, this cinema will cease to operate.'

The print was so minute, one almost needed a magnifying glass to read it, and it seemed such an inadequate epitaph for a picture house that had provided the picture-going public of Uxbridge with thirty-nine years of entertainment.

The Savoy was soon acquired by Ladbrokes, who converted the auditorium into a bingo hall and the second floor into a casino-type social club. The message proclaimed by the new owners across the front of the canopy was 'You'll love it at Ladbrokes'. But it is debatable whether the filmgoers of the previous four decades would have agreed. However, even the new craze for bingo couldn't last forever, and the building was demolished in May 1983, the corner site currently being occupied by the Royal Bank of Scotland.

MIGHTY! MIGHTY!! MIGHTY!!!

The Greatest War Film Ever Screened

STARKLY
REALISTIC.

REAL WAR.

DRAMA, THRILL
AND COMEDY,
IN THE
FRONT LINE.

TANKS, MUD,
MEN, GUNS,
AS THE
TOMMIES
KNEW IT.

MEN FROM EAST,
WEST, NORTH,
SOUTH,
MEET ON
THE SOMME.

A NEW ERA PRODUCTION.
By Permission of
The Army Council

EXPERIENCE WHAT
REAL WAR MEANS
BY SEEING
THE SOMME.

FROM FACTORY
AND FIELD, FROM
MOUNTAIN AND
MILL, FROM
COTTAGE AND
CASTLE, CAME THE
MEN WHO FOUGHT
ON THE SOMME.

"MONS" WAS THE
ARMY'S WAR;

THE SOMME WAS
EVERYBODY'S WAR

SHOWING

NOV. 21st and All the Week

: AT :

THE SAVOY THEATRE

UXBRIDGE

At 6.20 & 8.50 MONDAY, TUESDAY, THURSDAY & FRIDAY
And 3.50, 6.20 and 8.50 WEDNESDAY and SATURDAY

An example of the kind of newspaper advertising that the cinema used only for epic or 'blockbuster' films.

Cinema advertising in a local shop, c. 1930. The poster in W.H. Smith's window is for *The Broadway Melody* showing at the Savoy, just two doors away. The notice underneath reads 'Read the book of the film at the Savoy', and the side window is full of copies.

The Savoy cinema in the early 1930s, its entrance hidden by the High Street traffic congestion.

A side view of the Uxbridge Savoy taken in August 1934. The film advertised on the billboard is a reissue of *The W Plan*, starring Madeleine Carroll and first shown at the Savoy in 1931. The author of the book on which the film was based was at the time living in Court Drive, Hillingdon. He was Lt-Col. Graham Seton Hutchison, who wrote under the name Graham Seton.

The narrow but attractive foyer of the Savoy as it looked in 1937. The poster on the left showing Anna Lee in *OHMS* omits the name of her co-star John (now Sir John) Mills. An unusual feature is the weighing machine to the left of the auditorium doors.

A late 1937 photograph of the Savoy, when still under the ownership of Union Cinemas.

This interior shot taken from the circle of the Savoy gives an indication of the narrowness of the auditorium.

A view of the Savoy auditorium as seen from the stage.

Newspaper advertisement for *Edison The Man*, the film being screened on the night the Savoy was bombed in November 1940.

The last picture of the Savoy as a cinema in June 1960.

It took an army of 350 workmen just twenty-two weeks to complete the construction of the town's most majestic cinema – the Regal – at the upper end of the High Street. Built on the site originally known as Park Lodge Estate, which included the 'largest oak tree in Middlesex', it was the latest addition to the Abrahams family's cinemas. Three years earlier, in 1928, A.E. Abrahams had opened the first of his Regal circuit at Marble Arch, the first British independent cinema in the West End. His son, D.A. Abrahams, personally supervised every stage of the building work at Uxbridge, carried out by L.F. Richardson of Streatham.

The task of designing the Regal was entrusted to Maidenhead based architect E. Norman Bailey, who was responsible for the large Adelphi in Slough, and other houses in Maidenhead and Reading. But it is for his exotic, flamboyant, Art Deco design of the Regal that he will be remembered. As a result of his work, especially on the auditorium, the Department of the Environment listed the cinema as a Grade II building of historic and architectural interest in November 1976. In October 2000, this listing was elevated to Grade II* status, a grade enjoyed by only four per cent of all listed buildings in England.

But despite the sumptuous grandeur of the interior décor, Mr Bailey's design for the Regal's frontage was, of necessity, quite a modest one. The entrance, measuring a mere 15 yards, was squeezed into the middle of a row of terraced shops, and gave no indication of what lay beyond the main doors. The façade, often described as Egyptian style (probably because of the lettering employed for the name 'Regal'), was finished in 'Hathernware' medium glazed faience tiling with tasteful touches of colour along the top. And in their souvenir brochure produced for the opening, the owners wrote: 'In designing the front elevation to the High Street, the architect had endeavoured to add a touch of brightness to this end of Uxbridge'.

Inside the main foyer, Bailey's artistry began to manifest itself as patrons

August 1931 – and only the bare framework is in position as work on the Regal, Uxbridge, has not long started. It is difficult to believe that four months later, the now listed building celebrated its opening.

A page from the souvenir brochure produced for the opening of the Regal in December 1931.

The **REGAL**
UXBRIDGE,
Opened
December
1 9 3 1

FOREWORD

TO-DAY, Uxbridge and the vicinity is a rapidly developing and prosperous town : its population sophisticated and appreciating a degree of luxury and entertainment which, hitherto, was only to be found in the West End of London.

Our object in building THE REGAL, UXBRIDGE, was to bring that West End entertainment and environment to your door—not only that, but to give you an entertainment which, to-day, is within the means of every purse.

You are the best judge of whether we have succeeded in this object. If we have, we will value your continued patronage, but if we have fallen short of your expectations, we invite your criticism : it will help us to attain perfection.

At all times we will continue to offer you the highest form of entertainment obtainable in the British Isles.

The Regal is owned by Messrs. Regal (Uxbridge) Limited, 25, Shaftesbury Avenue, London, W.1.

encountered a spacious vestibule, elegantly decorated with brilliant cut mirrors, terrazzo flooring and subtle ceiling and wall lighting. A wide, two-way staircase led to a landing at the halfway stage, then a second flight went up to another foyer known as the 'crush hall'. This low-ceilinged area housed secondary pay boxes, the main one being sited outside the front entrance, and doors leading to offices, the car park and auditorium. The two auditorium doors, and another two on a higher level, led to a magnificent arena, laid out in stadium style. Instead of a balcony, the seating accommodation of 1,700 was tiered in a graceful gradient from the rear wall to the stage. And all around was evidence of the architect's *pièce de résistance*. The dominant feature was an elaborately adorned ceiling in which cleverly concealed lighting revealed a majestic sweep of contours from the projection box down to the uniquely curved proscenium arch. The walls and doorways in particular were decorated with an intricate network of patterns reminiscent of the oriental style. On the first floor, the complex also incorporated a fully licensed café (the biggest in Uxbridge at the time) and a ballroom.

The owners, justifiably proud of their enterprise, had apparently been rather reticent in releasing advance information about the auditorium, preferring to wait for the public reaction on the opening day. Confident what the verdict would be, and that the building would speak for itself, they dispensed with the usual official opening ceremony and did not invite a well-known celebrity, as was often the custom.

On Boxing Day afternoon in 1931 (a Saturday), long queues formed outside the cinema in anticipation of the opening performance, and once inside, the full house was

UXBRIDGE LUXURY CINEMA

your
REGAL
programme

september, 1933

Front cover of the detailed, illustrated monthly programme issued free by the Regal during the 1930s. By the end of the decade, the usherettes' costumes differed quite considerably from the one depicted.

treated to an exhibition of multicoloured lighting effects before the programme began. After the National Anthem was played on the Compton organ by the Regal's first organist, Tom Walker, the whole of the auditorium was fully lit for the first time, and its exciting effect was greeted with a spontaneous ovation from the appreciative audience. Then it was down to the main business of showing films, and the programme consisted of a newsreel, two shorts, Laurel and Hardy in *Laughing Gravy*, an organ interlude, and finally the feature film *Reaching for the Moon* with Douglas Fairbanks Snr (whom the audience heard speak on screen for the first time), Bebe Daniels and a young Bing Crosby who sang only one song.

After the performance, Mr Abrahams Snr hosted a tea and cocktail party for the prominent members of the community, while outside, crowds were already gathering for the second house. During its first year, the Regal attracted 750,000 customers, paying admission prices from 6d to 2s 6d.

Soon after its opening, the cinema initiated stage shows to accompany the films, and there were changes of programme every Monday and Thursday. The stage acts ranged from comedians and singers to musicians and full-scale dance bands. By the mid to late thirties the Regal was booking top liners including the Western Brothers, Clapham and Dwyer, Leslie Hutchinson ('Hutch'), Turner Layton, Elsie and Doris Waters, Beryl Orde, Troise and his Mandoliers, and the Billy Cotton and Roy Fox bands.

Full use was made of the John Compton organ which, having no lift, was permanently positioned in the centre of the orchestra pit with the console connected to two specially constructed organ chambers behind a decorative grille to the left of the stage. During the thirties, many celebrated organists played at the Regal, among them Alex Taylor, Jack Ferguson, Gordon Spicer, Bobby Pagan and Brian Trant. Crosbie Scott was a regular from 1939 to 1942, followed by Matt Ross until 1946. Another attraction provided by the cinema in 1938 was their service of bringing iced fruit drinks and afternoon tea to patrons in their seats, who could place their orders on the way in. This was of course, in addition to the chocolates and ice creams sold by the spotlighted usherettes during the interval. The adjoining café and ballroom were always popular and, apart from private lettings, the Regal held its own Dance Seasons. In September 1933, the price of a dinner and dance ticket was 3s 6d, which also included a London Dance Band and Cabaret. The ballroom was also used regularly for dancing lessons.

Within a few years of its opening, the cinema, like many other independent houses, was leased to the Union Cinemas group, which in turn was taken over by ABC in 1937, at the same time as the Savoy and the Marlborough in nearby Yiewsley. But a year or so before the changeover, the children's Union Cinema Club had been formed for youngsters to attend their own Saturday morning performances. Known as the 'tuppenny rush' for obvious reasons, they attracted enormous crowds who queued outside a rarely-used side entrance near the rear of the cinema. I was one of them.

For our tuppence, we saw a main feature – invariably a B Western featuring Buck Jones, Ken Maynard or Bob Steele, a cartoon, and most importantly, a ten minute chapter of the current serial. Notable serials that spring to mind include *Undersea*

A 1937 photograph of the impressive Regal frontage, when the pay box was situated on the pavement outside. Eventually it was relocated in the vestibule.

Kingdom and *The Vigilantes are Coming* (a title that was changed for our benefit to *The Mounties are Coming*, on the assumption – probably correct – that we would not know the word 'vigilantes'), *The Fighting Marines*, *Adventures of Rex and Rinty* and *Blake of Scotland Yard*. And two enjoyable main features were *Dick Turpin* and *Emil and the Detectives*.

Another item always included in the programme was community singing accompanied by the organ. The words of the songs were projected on to the screen with the familiar 'bouncing ball' along the top. Popular favourites at the time included 'Roll Along Covered Wagon', 'South of the Border', 'Red Sails in the Sunset' and 'Chapel in the Moonlight'. The singing ended with the Union Club members' own song, to the tune of the march 'Blaze Away'. Members had their own badges and were known as 'Union Chums'. After the takeover, the Saturday morning shows continued for the next four decades, but now the youngsters were called the ABC Minors, as was the club. The mixture was mostly as before, but the words of their song were amended to incorporate the new title, although the tune remained the same.

The organ accompaniment from 1966 to 1973 was provided by local organist Arthur Critchley who described to me in detail some of his experiences while playing for the Saturday morning matinées. I gathered that the 500 or more children were not his favourite audience, as the din they created sometimes drowned the mighty organ, while they pelted him with missiles into the bargain. In particular, he dreaded the conker season which he said could be highly dangerous, and he recounted how 'one day, a soggy, wet peach stone landed on my music, sliding down onto the music stand. I was not amused and hurled it back at the offender, much to the general delight, and a riot ensued.' He also remembered 'one little darling who leaned over the orchestra pit rail and made a balloon squeak in time with the music.' Arthur told me that occasionally he would stay on after the show, and unwind by serenading the cleaners for an hour before the afternoon programme started.

During the Second World War, the Regal, like most cinemas nationwide, continued to enjoy good business, and when the house was full, as it often was, the signboard reading 'Queuing All Parts' was much in evidence. This was probably never more true than on 6 September 1942, when the long-awaited epic *Gone with the Wind* was generally released, almost three years after its Atlanta première. Today of course, it would be referred to as a 'blockbuster'. All cinemas were obliged to increase their prices for the run of the film that was booked for a fortnight instead of the usual week, thereby creating a bit of history for the Regal, although some other cinemas did follow suit. For the first week, most seats had to be booked in advance, but for the second, there were 1,600 unreserved seats at every performance. Admission prices were 2s 6d, 3s and 4s.

Over the years, the cinema has served as a venue for various functions other than showing films. Probably the most notable was when it was chosen for the Uxbridge Charter Day ceremony on 18 May 1955. This was a royal charter granting the town borough status, with the ceremony being performed by the Duchess of Kent. The roof of the front canopy was bedecked with flags and bunting, and a red carpet laid out in front of the entrance for the royal party, the Duchess being accompanied by her

MONDAY
MAY 17th

The "Middlesex Advertiser and County Gazette"

IN CONJUNCTION WITH

UNION CINEMAS LTD.

WILL PRESENT AT THE

UNION CINEMA'S REGAL UXBRIDGE

THREE TIMES DAILY FOR THE WHOLE WEEK

UXBRIDGE CORONATION SOUND FILM REVIEW

SHOWING HOW UXBRIDGE CELEBRATED THE CORONATION OF H.M. KING GEORGE VI.

AND ALSO THIS FILM WILL BE SHOWN THE FOLLOWING WEEK AT THE

UNION CINEMA'S MARLBORO' YIEWSLEY

THIS FILM, AFTER ITS SHOWING WILL BE PRESENTED, IN A GOLDEN CASKET, TO THE TOWN AS A SOUVENIR OF THE CORONATION OF MAY 12th, 1937.

A local newspaper announcement regarding an important national event in 1937.

daughter, Princess Alexandra, and son, the Duke of Kent. Other less illustrious occasions included the use of the theatre by local scout and guide troops for Empire Day celebrations, and special events such as fashion shows staged by the management in the late forties and early fifties.

In May 1963, the Regal hosted the month-long Uxbridge Festival of Arts, which featured concerts by the Hallé Orchestra, conducted by Sir John Barbirolli, the RAF Central Band and the band of the U.S.A.A.F.. A similar event followed two years later and the Hayes Girls' Choir performed a concert there in December 1966.

Throughout the 1970s, the National Theatre Organ Club presented a series of organ concerts, the final one being held in March 1976. But four years earlier, on 29 January 1972, Arthur Critchley had played the Compton organ for the last time at a children's matinée, and shortly afterwards, the ABC group ruled that it would no longer be played at any film performances.

By 1977, audiences had dwindled disastrously, and the cinema closed its doors for the last time on 4 November, with the screening of *Demon Seed* and *The Super Cops*. Hardly a very dignified end for the aptly named Regal, which, in its heyday, had fed its patrons a steady diet of box office successes that included *Treasure Island*, *A Tale of Two Cities*, *Rose Marie*, *Mutiny on the Bounty*, *Captains Courageous*, *The Adventures of Robin Hood*, *You Can't Take it With You*, *The Wizard of Oz*, *Gone with the Wind*, *Mr Smith Goes to Washington*, *They Died With Their Boots On* (for which I queued over two hours on Whit Monday 1942), *Mrs Miniver*, *Yankee Doodle Dandy*, *Casablanca*, *Quo Vadis*, *Ben Hur* and *My Fair Lady*. Among the galaxy of stars on view were the Marx brothers, Mickey Rooney and Judy Garland, Bette Davis, Gene Kelly, Frank Sinatra, Elizabeth

The Regal's ground floor vestibule with staircase up to a second foyer. The doorway and stairs on the left led up to the café and ballroom.

Taylor, Doris Day and James Dean.

The Regal remained empty for seven years, reopening as a snooker hall in 1984, utilizing the former ballroom and café. Then an application was approved to convert the auditorium into a nightclub, but because of the Department of the Environment's decision to grant listed building status, the interior décor has, thankfully, been preserved intact. As the backstage area at the rear of the building is currently being used as a health and fitness club, the whole complex represents a multipurpose leisure centre for playing snooker, drinking, dancing, keeping fit and working out. Not exactly what the creators of the 'dream palace' had in mind when they built it over seventy years ago!

The illuminated console of the Regal's Compton organ.

Side view of the Regal auditorium, showing the stadium-style seating, the Art Deco ceiling, and the curvaceous proscenium arch.

Another side view of the Regal interior, which highlights the ornate décor above the exit doors.

Newspaper advertisement for the long awaited classic *Gone With The Wind*. Premièred in Atlanta, Georgia in December 1939, it did not arrive on our local screens until September 1942.

20	Theatre—	1
19	Date Card No.	2
18	12-7-53	3
17	Minor's Name	4
	Gloria Sloanes	
16	Date of Birth	5
	Jan 3rd. 1946	
15		6
14	ABC MINORS	7
13		8
12	**PLEASE BRING THIS CARD**	9
11	**and** **WEAR YOUR MINORS BADGE**	10

Gloria Mulleney (née Sloanes)'s membership card for the Regal's ABC Minor's Club. She was not really old enough to join, but lied about her age!

Charter Day, 1955. Standing on the red carpet in front of the Regal entrance is the Duchess of Kent, with the mayor, Mr James Cochrane. Her son and daughter can just be seen beneath the canopy.

An attentive audience watches as the Duchess presents Uxbridge with its charter granting borough status.

UXBRIDGE FESTIVAL OF ARTS 1–31 MAY 1963

Sir John Barbirolli with the Hallé Orchestra
The Barrow Poets Wilfred Brown and John Williams
Humphrey Lyttelton George Malcolm
John Ogdon Evelyn Rothwell with the Alberni Quartet
Marion Studholme with the Central Band of the
Royal Air Force
The Band of the U.S.A.A.F.

Architecture Art Books Choral music Films
Floral art Handicrafts Modelling Opera
Organ music Photography Plays Printing Waterways

Illustrated Programme Two Shillings and Sixpence

Front cover of the Uxbridge Festival of Arts Programme for 1963. The main events were staged at the Regal cinema, and another similar festival followed in 1965, featuring the Royal Philharmonic Orchestra.

A view of the Regal auditorium from the stage. Seated at the console of the Compton organ is the late Mr Bernard Leno, who voluntarily maintained the organ after the cinema had closed.

The Regal frontage, photographed a few years before its closure. Since then, it has appeared in the background of a number of TV films, including Agatha Christie's *The ABC Murders*.

One of the last pictures of the Regal interior, depicting the majestic Art Deco of the auditorium. The wide screen has replaced the original format (4:3 aspect ratio).

The Regal's last manageress, Mrs Winifred Bishop, pictured outside the cinema in October 1977, just before it closed. Back in 1936, another lady manager, Ruth Clark, was appointed, and the press reported that she was the first woman in Uxbridge to hold such an important managerial position.

The Regal frontage as it is today. Only the canopy with its new title has been changed – and, of course, the posters.

A rear view of the Regal as it is today. Instead of cinema billboards, the advertising is for a Health and Fitness Club, which shares the building with a discotheque and nightclub.

In August 1937, the local press reported that plans had been approved for the building of a new luxury cinema on the Hillingdon Road at Hillingdon Heath. It had been designed by a Russian architect, A.V. Pilichowsky, and would accommodate 1,350 people. By a strange coincidence, the artist's impression reproduced in the *Middlesex Advertiser* bore a remarkable resemblance to the future Uxbridge Odeon, although admittedly the frontage appeared larger and more luxurious. However, nothing more was heard of the project, and a few months later building work began on the Odeon. Had the plans come to fruition, the Hillingdon cinema was destined to be named the 'Gloria' which I believe would have been a first in cinema nomenclature.

In June 1937, while the proposals for the Hillingdon cinema were still being discussed, an old hotel, the Brookfield, and an adjoining house known as Hurstlea, at the western end of the High Street, were demolished. And although the site remained derelict for a while, work soon began on Uxbridge's newest and largest cinema, the Odeon. This was the latest addition to the rapidly expanding empire founded by the legendary Oscar Deutsch. Throughout the thirties, Deutsch had built 140 new cinemas nationwide, in addition to acquiring almost as many existing ones. Odeons were built in a distinctive style and represented a departure from the flamboyant and sometimes over-decorative Chinese or Moorish designs. Nevertheless, they were excellent examples of sleek, streamlined architecture, having their exteriors faced with large cream-coloured faience tiles and their corners smoothly rounded. Many featured a slim-line tower or fin, often producing a ship-like appearance.

The Uxbridge building was designed by Andrew Mather and his associate Keith Roberts. Mather was one of Deutsch's principal architects, along with Harry Weedon and George Coles, and in conjunction with Roberts, was responsible for another ten Odeons in 1938 alone.

The square, box-like exterior lacked the curved streamlining of many elegant Odeons built during the decade, but the frontage did include a tower and fin bearing the distinctive Odeon lettering at one end of the building. At the opposite end, a single giant black column gave the impression that it was supporting a large portion of the structure on its own.

The interior decoration, in keeping with the Odeon style, was on plain rather than fancy lines, employing a colour scheme of warm tones of brown, blue and gold. The auditorium had been designed to create a spacious, modernistic effect, and the plush, upholstered armchair seats with their extra leg space added a touch of luxury. There were 1,215 of them in the stalls and another 622 in the balcony.

The main entrance to the theatre was set back from the main road, allowing for a covered drive-in to the front steps. These led into a circular vestibule with a pay box in the centre, and entrances to the auditorium, balcony and offices all leading off. The main wall of the staircase to the circle was decorated with illustrated panels depicting Uxbridge and its activities, past and present, and the stairs led to a second, larger foyer that even included a miniature garden. The total cost of the building, which incorporated upstairs offices and three shops built into the frontage, was £50,400.

The local press announcement of the Odeon opening read 'Grand Opening Ceremony' and grand it certainly was – the most impressive by far of any cinema in the district, and for that matter, any other neighbouring area. The date was Monday 20

June 1938, and all seats had been sold in advance. It is interesting to note that the newspaper report of 17 June described the advent of the Odeon as 'a definite step forward in the development and modernization of the High Street of this ancient township'. Interesting, that is, when compared with the editorial in the *Middlesex Advertiser and Gazette* exactly a year earlier when the writer considered that cinemas in general 'would usurp the sites of beautiful mansions and their gardens'. He went on with particular reference to the proposed building of the Odeon: 'and we now have the prospect of a multiple cinema combine with its hard, garish and modernistic style occupying a site that represented a gracious age that is passing away'. The reference was, of course to Brookfield and Hurstlea. But history repeats itself, and nowadays cinema enthusiasts complain that beautiful picture houses have been replaced by garish supermarkets and the like.

On the opening night, large crowds lined the pavements long before the doors opened at 7.15 p.m. The Gaumont British News Company was in attendance, giving the occasion considerable coverage in its newsreel during the following week. Commentator E.V.H. Emmett described the cinema as 'one more palatial building in the familiar Odeon style' and the celebrities 'as distinguished an audience as ever attended a first night.'

The identity of the film chosen for the opening had been kept a closely guarded secret right up until the last moment, being advertised as a 'Special Presentation of a Great British Production'. It was, in fact, Alexander Korda's empire epic *The Drum*, made a couple of miles down the road from the Odeon at Denham Studios. The picture had already enjoyed a lavish première at Odeon's flagship cinema in Leicester Square

The auditorium of the Uxbridge Odeon, with its futuristic, almost 'space-age' look. This is an early picture taken before the cinema opened in 1938 – and before the installation of the familiar octagonal shaped Odeon wall clocks.

Another early photograph of the Odeon interior, taken from the stage.

when the author of the book, A.E.W. Mason, addressed the audience, but the Uxbridge showing represented a provincial première – a 'sneak preview'. Since most of the cinemas in the area opened with fairly run of the mill films, the showing of an important picture like *The Drum* was unique, quite apart from the surprise element and the glitzy array of celebrities present. First of these to arrive was the star of *The Drum*, Sabu, who came dressed in the colourful costume he wore in the film. He was followed by his co-star Valerie Hobson, and then Anna Neagle with her husband Herbert Wilcox. The programme started with 45 minutes of music from the Central Band of the RAF, after which the pipers of the King's Own Scottish Borderers marched through the auditorium to the stage. A retinue of distinguished guests including the Odeon chief Oscar Deutsch, Mrs Deutsch and the architect Andrew Mather followed them. The cinema was then declared opened by the Chairman of Uxbridge UDC, H.A. Leno.

The Drum was screened for one night only, and the rest of the week was devoted to *Something to Sing About* starring James Cagney. Those of us who were not fortunate enough to book tickets in advance for the opening had to wait until the film returned to the Odeon on general release. These was one consolation, however: Valerie Hobson made a second personal appearance when she paid a return visit on the first night, Monday 24 October.

Saturday 10 September saw the birth of the Odeon's 'Mickey Mouse Club' for junior filmgoers. Admission was 3d (a penny dearer than the Regal), and members were issued with badges. One young member, Ken Pearce, now a local historian, remembers watching a Buck Rogers twelve-part serial and another entitled *Flaming Frontiers*. He told me that he had 'never quite forgiven Hitler for preventing me from seeing the end of that gripping drama'. He was referring to the closure of cinemas on 3 September 1939, with the final episode still to be screened. However, I was able to reveal to Ken that the hero (Johnny Mack Brown) came through unscathed in the last chapter. Surprise, surprise!

In later years the name of the junior film circle was changed to the Odeon Cinema Club (or OCC) and members had their own song, which went as follows:

'Is everybody happy? Yes!
Do we ever worry? No!
To the Odeon we have come
Now we're all together
We can have some fun
Do we ask for favours? No!
Do we love our neighbours? Yes!
We're a hundred thousand strong
So how can we all be wrong?
As members of the OCC we stress
Is everybody happy? Yes!'

During its first year, the Odeon booked a succession of 'classic' films including *The Hurricane*, *Snow White and the Seven Dwarfs*, *The Adventures of Marco Polo*, *Sixty Glorious Years*, *The Adventures of Tom Sawyer* and *The Lady Vanishes*. And on Monday 4 September, 1939, another Alexander Korda picture *The Four Feathers* was due to be shown, but the outbreak of war on the previous day put paid to that. Fortunately, the film was postponed for only a fortnight, eventually opening on 18 September. The female star of *The Four Feathers*, June Duprez, had been billed to make a personal appearance on 4 September, but she made up her enforced absence just two months later, when I saw her appear on the same Odeon stage on 27 November in conjunction with the showing of her latest film *The Lion Has Wings*. This propaganda picture had been produced at Denham in a record shooting time of twelve days.

In the early part of the Second World War, the Odeon staged a number of Sunday afternoon charity concerts, and the guest stars willingly gave their services free of charge. One that I attended on 20 October 1940 was in aid of the local Spitfire Fund, and Oscar Deutsch had generously allowed the theatre to be used at no cost. Stars appearing included Great Gynt, Valerie Hobson and David Tree, with radio and music hall comedian Leonard Henry acting as compere. Marie Lohr and Rex Harrison were also expected to attend, but sent a message of apology for their absence due to filming on *Major Barbara* at Denham. In wartime, Sunday was often a working day due to actors' service and war work commitments. In fact, during a question and answer session with the audience in one part of the show, David Tree, resplendent in dark suit and black bowler, was asked by a young lad why he wasn't in the army. He replied that he had been granted special leave to work on *Major Barbara*, and would be rejoining his unit during the following week. This was greeted with loud applause.

Other concerts followed; some featuring the RAF Dance Orchestra (The Squadronaires) led by Sgt Jimmy Miller, which was stationed in Uxbridge. Meanwhile,

Read the Local Film News each week in the "Advertiser-Gazette"

FREE CAR PARK

—MONDAY, JUNE 20th—

DOORS OPEN 7.15

GRAND
OPENING CEREMONY

BY

H. A. LENO, Esq., J.P.

(CHAIRMAN, UXBRIDGE U.D.C.)

•

SPECIAL ENGAGEMENT OF THE

BAND OF H.M. ROYAL AIR FORCE

(BY PERMISSION OF THE AIR COUNCIL)

Squadron Leader R. P. O'Donnell, M.V.O., Director of Music, R.A.F.

•

ON THE SCREEN

SPECIAL PRESENTATION OF A GREAT BRITISH PRODUCTION

(By courtesy of London Film Productions Ltd.)

FULL SUPPORTING PROGRAMME

SEATS MAY BE RESERVED FOR THIS GREAT OCCASION ONLY.

THEATRE BOOKING OFFICE NOW OPEN— BUT BOOK EARLY!

THE ODEON IS OPPOSITE THE TROLLEY-BUS TERMINUS AT THE BOTTOM OF THE HIGH ST.

Local newspaper announcement for the opening of the Odeon in 1938.

the glut of good films continued: *Goodbye Mr Chips*, *The Spy in Black*, *Three Smart Girls Grow Up*, *Stagecoach*, *Wuthering Heights*, *The Stars Look Down*, *The Grapes of Wrath* and *The Great Dictator*.

The Odeon management showed considerable enterprise in promoting their 'product'. In October 1939, when I saw *The Mikado*, the audience was invited to applaud after every musical number, and if the volume warranted it, the scene would be reprised, as an encore. It was a novel idea but on some occasions the film's original running time was much extended, which may not have appealed to people with buses to catch. Other ideas included vestibule displays when *The Mark of Zorro* and *The Thief of Baghdad* were playing in 1941. Props used in these pictures were exhibited in showcases, as were some from *The Black Swan* in 1943. As a prelude to the last showing each evening of *Phantom of the Opera*, a projectionist clad in a black cloak slunk across

Newspaper advertisement for *The Drum* in October 1938. No surprise this time, as the film was on general release.

Newspaper advertisement for *The Four Feathers* in 1939, with an ominous date at the top – Sunday 3 September. The outbreak of war caused a fortnight's postponement.

the stage as the curtains opened.

This was the era of smartly turned out usherettes and commissionaires. Oscar Deutsch had decreed that all Odeon staff nationwide should maintain the highest standards of smartness, and Uxbridge was no exception. Former chief usherette Barbara Hill and her friend and colleague Doreen Bromfield described their daily routine as regimental. Long before opening time, the staff lined up on parade every day for inspection by the manager and head usherette, when everything was checked from fingernails down to the seams of their stockings. Torches and cigarette lighters (for lighting patrons' cigarettes) had to be switched on to prove they were working, and in addition the girls were expected to answer any questions, technical and otherwise, that the customers might ask. Barbara and Doreen still remember the answers such as the size of the screen, length of 'throw' or beam from projection box to screen, seating capacity, number and position of deaf-aid seats, and so on. And all for £2 a week (in 1946), eventually increasing to £3 2s 6d. The average working day started at 1 p.m. and finished at 10.30 p.m., and the girls were given one day off a week, plus two 'early nights'.

From the way Barbara and Doreen talked about the happy family atmosphere that prevailed among the staff, from the manager down, it was obvious that they loved every minute of their time at the Odeon. This is borne out in an article in the circuit's house magazine *The Circle* in 1946, which described the 'family spirit' at Uxbridge and included nine pictures of the staff. Some of the girls' best-remembered moments related to celebrity visits. Actors who lived locally attended quite regularly, among them Valerie Hobson, Jimmy Hanley, Finlay Currie (who always gave the usherette a shilling tip) and Sir John Mills. On one occasion, Sir John brought his daughter Juliet, and Doreen remembers with great pride how she escorted them to the manager's office after they had watched the film *The October Man*, in which they played father and daughter. A year later, Doreen was chosen to present a bouquet on stage to Edana Romney when she came to promote her film *Corridor of Mirrors*. But at the last minute, she developed stage fright, and was allowed to make the presentation in the foyer instead.

Despite the decline in cinema attendance, sparked off in the 1960s, the Odeon, together with the Regal, had struggled on well into the '70s. Then, in 1976, in keeping with the current trend of dividing cinemas into two or three auditoria, the Odeon chain decided to 'triple' their Uxbridge house which, after the alterations, reopened on 25 April with *The Man Who Would Be King*, *Farewell My Lovely* and *Return of the Pink Panther*. Unfortunately, the changeover failed to solve the problem of the missing millions, and only succeeded in granting the cinema a stay of execution for a further six years, until it came under the axe in 1982. Its demolition in 1984, after it had stood empty for two years, marked the end of an era, as Uxbridge was now without a cinema for the first time in over seventy years.

But the Odeon story did not end there, for in 1990, the wheel turned full circle when the Rank Organization, who had acquired the circuit after Oscar Deutsch's death in 1941, decided that the time was ripe to build a second Odeon on the old site. A spokesman said there had been a great resurgence of interest in cinema since 1985, and admissions were still rising. So, like a phoenix from the ashes, a new albeit much smaller building arose, housing only two screens with accommodation for 439 patrons in one auditorium and 230 in the other. Despite its size, the building incorporated a licensed bar, refreshment area and viewing galleries for the disabled in both cinemas. A computerized booking office in the main foyer allowed customers to book seats in advance. The opening night, Thursday 12 July 1990, featured a charity performance of *Back to the Future 3*, a day earlier than the film's general release, and on the following afternoon the cinema opened to the general public with *Music Box* showing in the second auditorium.

But the cinema's days were numbered, and this time it was due to soaring, not falling attendances. In 2000, UK admissions totalled 142 million, with Odeon claiming the largest market share at 26 per cent. In February, Rank had sold out to Cinven (already the owners of the ABC circuit) and now it was Odeon's intention 'to be the UK's most dynamic cinema brand', in other words to build bigger and better cinemas. So with a new £5 million multiplex project planned in a shopping centre development named The Chimes, there was obviously no further need for the little building at the opposite end of the High Street.

The opening of the new multiplex on 9 March 2001 must have been some sort of record in that the town had been home to three Odeons (four if one counts the 'tripled' building). It is reached by escalators within the shopping complex and by stairs at the rear entrance. The cinema comprises nine screens, all equipped with Dolby Digital surround sound, a café and bar, and five box office points. The largest auditorium seats 418, the smallest 195 and all are set out in stadium style.

Cover of the magazine programme for *The Four Feathers*, showing John Clements and June Duprez.

Interior décor is quite plain, in complete contrast to the dream palaces of yesteryear, although I sensed a general feeling of comfort and luxury on a recent tour of the building, courtesy of the young, enthusiastic manager, Tim Ripley. And anyone could not help being impressed on entering the vast projection area, where nine state of the art projectors service the nine screens simultaneously. But there was no projectionist in sight, although Mr Ripley assured me there was one on call, should the need arise.

On 8 March 2001, a day before opening to the general public, the new Odeon staged a gala night which was attended by TV presenters Melanie Sykes and Toby Anstis. Also present were Sarah van de Burgh (of *Neighbours* fame) and a detachment of US marines. The cinema's policy is to show a wide range of films to suit all ages from children to senior citizens. It also includes 'art house' and 'Bollywood' pictures. Discounts are available for students and seniors; children's parties may be arranged in the café and the inevitable popcorn is very much in evidence.

Future prospects for the new multiplex are looking good, as after only six months of business, it figured in a list of the top ten Odeons in the country with the highest number of admissions.

Newspaper advertisement for *The Lion Has Wings* in November 1939. One of the stars of the film, June Duprez, made a personal appearance on the Odeon stage in the evening.

A group picture of the Uxbridge Odeon staff in 1947, including deputy manager Mr Formby, secretary Olive Hopkins and manager Mr Frisby-Smith in the centre of the front row.

The Odeon usherettes and cashiers photographed with the mayoress in 1947. Head usherette Barbara Simpson is third from the left in the front row, and her friend Doreen Williams is on the extreme right of the back row.

The daily staff inspection of the Odeon usherettes, *c.* 1948, in their dark green uniforms, pillbox caps and silver shoes. Head usherette Barbara Simpson, having checked that the girls' torches are all working, now examines their silk stockings to ensure the seams are straight.

Four of the Odeon usherettes relaxing in their staff room during a tea break. Head girl Barbara Simpson is tuning in to a wireless set presented to them by the Rank Organization as a reward for job performance.

A representative of the Rank Organization presenting the radio to the Odeon usherettes.

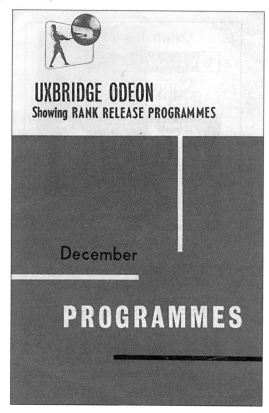

UXBRIDGE ODEON
Showing RANK RELEASE PROGRAMMES

December

PROGRAMMES

Front cover of the Odeon's illustrated
monthly programme for December 1962,
issued free to patrons.

One of the last pictures of the Uxbridge Odeon, taken in 1983.

Another view, taken during 1983, shortly before its closure.

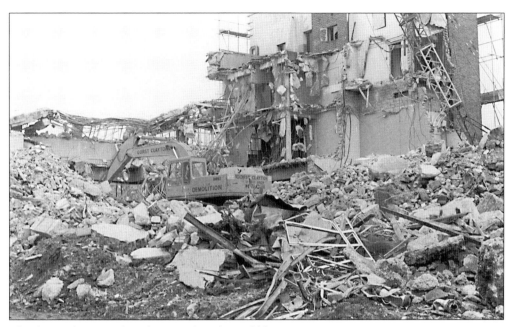

The former luxury Odeon being reduced to rubble in 1984.

The second Uxbridge Odeon, which rose up from the ashes of the first in 1990.

A presentation ceremony on the steps of the new, smaller Odeon. The manager, Mr Adrian Duffey, is on the extreme left.

A recent picture of Uxbridge's second Odeon closed and shuttered. Present plans are for its conversion to a Health Club.

Opening celebrations at the Uxbridge nine-screen Odeon in The Chimes in March 2001. Toby Anstis, Melanie Sykes and Sarah Van De Burgh are pictured with US Marines – and plenty of popcorn.

'Stairway to the Stars' – escalators lead up to the main entrance of the Odeon multiplex in 'The Chimes' shopping complex.

Two

Hayes: From Brotherhood to Bingo

It was almost three years after Jack Hutton's Rockingham Hall had opened in Uxbridge that the rapidly increasing population of Hayes was able to enjoy the new medium of silent movies. The town, which grew out of a small hamlet known as Botwell, had started to expand before the First World War. On the main GWR line from Paddington, it spawned a vast industrialized area, housing some of the best-known companies in the world. So the birth of the town's first cinema was not before its time.

Unfortunately, only scant records of the building and its specifications seem to have survived – nor are any photographs available. However, we know that the Middlesex County Council granted a cinematograph and music licence to the applicant, C.C. Spalding, in March 1913, and the cinema opened in early April. It was sited in a reasonably central position of the town in Station Road, and named quite simply 'Hayes Cinema'. A long white building all on one level with red velvet tip-up seats, it operated six nights a week, with the usual change of programme every Monday and Thursday. In addition to the evening performances, there were matinées on Wednesdays and Saturdays, and admission charges were 2d, 4d, 6d and 1d for children at matinées, when they received a complimentary bag of sweets. Occasionally the films were accompanied by a variety act. On Sundays the cinema was hired out to a religious group, the Botwell Brotherhood, who, starting on 13 April, held afternoon and evening meetings which helped supplement the hall's regular income. Not that the cinema needed subsidizing, for with the start of the First World War in 1914 more and more people flocked to the area to work in munitions, since many local factories were now engaged in 'war work'. Business appeared to be brisk from the beginning and consequently the cinema did not need to advertise in the local press. Once again, as in Uxbridge, it was *Quo Vadis* which drew the biggest crowds. But by the end of 1915, the

Brotherhood built a new hall of its own, amid rumours that the building might be commandeered for the storage of war materials. So the cinema lost part of its income, but worse was to follow, for inexplicably it also lost virtually a captive audience, and came to an abrupt end in October 1916, when the building was converted into a restaurant. Seven years later, it became a Baptist tabernacle, when ironically, the projection box was used for magic lantern shows, and the old seating was still in place. Eventually, the Woolworth company acquired the building and their new store occupies the site today.

Somewhat surprisingly for a thriving township like Hayes, eight years elapsed before another cinema emerged – but the wait was worthwhile. For when it appeared, the Regent was acclaimed as the most up-to-date in the district. It was, of course, the only cinema in Hayes, and it is debatable whether it was superior to the Uxbridge Savoy, but for the local residents, it must have been a godsend. Certainly luxurious by comparison to the old Hayes Cinema hall, it was built only a matter of yards away, on the same side of Station Road. Flanked on both sides of its entrance by shop fronts, the Regent was a plain but pleasant-looking building, its narrow frontage comprising two square pillars clad with large tiles, and two low steps up to the main doors. Above the canopy bearing its name were three tall windows, and higher still, under a Romanesque-type top, the title 'Regent' was affixed to the brickwork.

The seating capacity was 834, including 140 in the balcony, although this was not

Newspaper advertisement for the opening of the first cinema in Hayes, combined with an announcement for the 'Brotherhood' organization who used the building on Sundays.

65

THE REGENT

CINEMA   HAYES

Phone: 167 HAYES.

For Best Pictures and Greatest Comfort.   *Most up-to-date House in the District*

A few minutes from Hayes Station.   Every Evening, 6 till 10.30.   Children's Matinee: Saturdays, at 2.30.   Prices of Admission: **6d., 9d., 1/3**

Monday, Tuesday, Wednesday, December 1st, 2nd, 3rd, 1924.

"THE ROYAL OAK"

A wonderful British Film of the time of the Roundheads and Cavaliers,
— FEATURING —
HENRY AINLEY, BETTY COMPSON and little PETER DEAR.

"SECRETS OF NATURE"

Something new in Nature Films, fascinating and instructive, entitled "CRABS & CAMOUFLAGE."

"EVE'S FILM REVUE"

Including the inimitable 'elix.

HAROLD LLOYD

in one of his laughter-provoking Comedies,

"EASY COME, EASY GO"

Thursday, Friday, Saturday, December 4th, 5th, 6th, 1924.

"WHAT PRICE LOVING CUP"

A Tale of the Turf, with
VIOLET HOPSON.

"SECRETS OF NATURE"

Of great interest to young and old.

LARRY SEMON

AS A

GROCER'S ASSISTANT.

"OUT OF THE INKWELL"

Cartoon Comedy.

Newspaper advertisement for the opening of the Regent cinema, Hayes, in 1924.

completed in time for opening. Seats were upholstered in fawn marquette with distinctive gold, saxe blue and black stripes. The cinema, whose owners were listed as Hayes Cinema Ltd, was at the time one of only a few picture houses that employed back projection.

Opening night was Monday 1 December 1924, with the screening of the British film *The Royal Oak* starring Betty Compson and Henry Ainley. In keeping with the then current trend, programmes changed on Mondays and Thursdays. Performances were confined to evenings, with a children's matinee on Saturdays; and admission prices were 6d, 9d and 1s 3d. The Regent incorporated a large stage, measuring 27ft by 40ft deep, which, in the early thirties, was used occasionally to provide an extra item to the film programme, as when the Hayes and Harlington Silver Prize Band performed there for a week in April 1932. The cinema was now advertising itself as the 'Regent Super Cinema – Where the Crowds Go'.

Many former Hayes residents have fond memories of picture-going at the Regent during the thirties, none more so than William K. Everson, distinguished cinema writer and historian, who hailed from nearby Cranford. Some years ago, I had the privilege of meeting Mr Everson (who by then had moved to New York) when he came over to give a lecture at the National Film Theatre. We discussed all the picture houses in the surrounding areas, and it became obvious that he had a soft spot for the Regent, which he described as the exclusive cinema of the first years of his movie-going life. He remembered the foyer, devoid of any frills or fancy décor; white marble stairs up to the balcony; and the café. As a young lad, he was a regular at the Saturday morning shows, and one of his most pleasurable memories was of the curtain (black with vertical lines of gold) rising to reveal the Mickey Mouse trademark at the start of the programme. By 1935, he was enjoying the more adult films, but as he said, the Regent was a young boy's paradise, as they showed so many Westerns and action films, plus Laurel and Hardy comedies, a fact borne out by many of my Hayes friends, who also have vivid memories of the Saturday serials.

Various changes had taken place at the cinema during the decade. Ownership had passed to a company called Broadmead Cinemas Ltd; seating capacity had been increased to 1,100; Western Electric Sound had been installed; and by 1937 admission prices were 9d and 2s. Still adventure films predominated: *The Road to Glory*, *OHMS*, *The Last of the Mohicans*, *China Seas* and *Elephant Boy*. Sadly, the Regent's days were numbered when, in 1938, plans were announced for the building of a new luxury cinema almost directly opposite. The competition would have proved too much, and consequently the old picture house was forced to close. It remained dark until the night of Monday 16 February 1948 when it reopened, this time as a theatre, with a production of Priestley's *When We are Married*. Since the 1920s, many old theatres and music halls throughout the country had been converted to picture palaces, but this was one of the rare examples of the situation in reverse. For the next six years, the theatre

The Regent in Station Road, Hayes,
c. 1937.

acted as a weekly repertory company, employing a host of actors and actresses who eventually became big names in films and television. Among them were Leo McKern, Terence Alexander, Kathleen Byron, John Le Mesurier, Patrick Cargill, Stanley Baker, Kenneth Williams, Diana Dors, Kay Kendall, Joan Sims, Anne Crawford, John McCallum, Donald Pleasance and Honor Blackman. There was also a young man who found fame as a playwright – his name was John Osborne. But while they all went on to greater glory, this was to be the final chapter of the Regent's history. The curtain came down on the last production in 1954, the inevitable demolition followed, and now the National Westminster Bank stands in its place.

From the time of its opening, the Regent had reigned supreme for almost nine years. As the only cinema in Hayes, it had the field to itself. That was until 1933, when a new rival – the Corinth – appeared on the scene. There was certainly scope for another picture house in the area, especially since the Corinth's location on the main Uxbridge Road at Hayes End was a considerable distance away from the Regent, on the opposite side of the town. Due to its proximity to a new large housing development, the Grange Park estate, the cinema had a ready-made audience. Both the estate and the cinema were built by Taylor Woodrow Ltd, who, at the opening, were congratulated on their initiative by the chairman of Hayes UDC – especially as it had provided work for a large number of men in the midst of the Depression.

Messrs J.M. Wilson and T. Elsom Hardy designed the Corinth for the proprietors F.J. Partner and Co., one of whose directors was Odeon chief Oscar Deutsch. The manager of the Odeon, Kingston-on-Thames, E. Colman, represented Mr Deutsch at the opening ceremony. He was accompanied by Myra Storm and Molly Hudson, who were described in the press report as 'two young ladies famous in the film industry'. Regrettably, no details of their fame are available.

The *Ideal Kinema and Studio* trade paper, dated 17 August 1933, described the

The former Regent cinema now operating as a theatre in the early 1950s.

Newspaper advertisement for the opening of the Corinth cinema, Hayes, in 1933.

architects' design of the exterior as 'imposing; finished in white cement; and modelled on bold, modern lines with a dominant feature of a large window and ornamental grille above the main entrance', while the local press wrote 'the bold, white front strikes a new note in cinema architecture, the simplicity and strong lines combining to give an attractive appearance.' Others might have considered the frontage to be rather plain. Six steps led up to the main entrance, beyond which were two vestibules – one a lofty foyer with green and gold décor, and the second a cosier 'crush hall'. The auditorium, which seated 808 all on one level, was decorated with restful shades of brown and gold, with a stippled orange dado around the side walls. The stage measured 34ft by 18ft deep, with main tabs in old gold with a green and red motif. An orchestra pit, two dressing rooms and a band room were also included in the complex.

Opening night was Saturday 5 August 1933. It had been a somewhat unusually sweltering start to the Bank Holiday weekend, and the invited guests and general public were impressed by the coolness of the interior. The programme started with music from the orchestra, followed by speeches, and finally the opening film *The Man from Toronto* starring Jessie Matthews. Supporting the main feature was Basil Rathbone in *After the Ball*, and as Sunday opening had recently been approved in the area, both films were played again on the following day. Subsequently programmes ran from Monday to Saturday, with a change on Sunday. According to newspaper advertisements, 'Thursday and Friday Nights are Surprise Nights'. Occasionally the Plaza Orchestra performed in addition to the films and, in October 1937 Ambrose and his band appeared on stage. Admission prices were 7d, 1s, 1s 6d and 2s.

The Corinth never enjoyed 'first-run' releases – most of its product being weeks if not months old. Eventually the management introduced a change of programme in mid-week, by which time children's Saturday morning shows were a regular feature. The cinema continued its policy in more or less the same vein until 1949, when it was acquired by the Essoldo circuit, and renamed the Essoldo. Then in 1954, it had the distinction of being the first picture house in the area to be equipped with the newly created Cinemascope screen, and although other local cinemas followed suit, the Essoldo remained the only one in the area with stereophonic sound. Among the notable 'scope films screened there were *The Robe* and its sequel *Demetrius and the Gladiators*, *The Man in the Grey Flannel Suit*, *Violent Saturday*, and *How to Marry a*

A view of the Corinth, Hayes, taken prior to its opening. Taylor Woodrow Ltd, whose estate office can be seen next door, were the builders of the cinema.

Millionaire. But by the end of the decade, the all-too-familiar story of falling attendances brought about the Essoldo's demise, and it closed on 8 July 1961, with a showing of *Return to Peyton Place*. Three months later the building was demolished, and replaced the year after by a multi-storey office block.

The new luxury picture palace across the street from the Regent which, in 1938, had caused that cinema's demise, was the Ambassador at the beginning of East Avenue. The building began life as a project of London and Southern Super Cinemas, but while it was still under construction, the Odeon circuit acquired the company. When it opened, the owners were listed as Hayes Ambassador Cinema Ltd, but after a year or so, it came under the Odeon umbrella, while always retaining its original name.

The Ambassador (which the locals eventually abbreviated to 'Ambass') was designed by architect F.C. Mitchell who incorporated a number of Odeon-style features in his plans. The main difference was that the majority of the exterior was brick-built, with the usual faience tiling confined to the fin and around the entrance. Despite being described in the local press as having simple, straight, modernist lines, the frontage featured a gracefully curved wall set back above the canopy. Rising from it, as the centrepiece, was a tall, square tower complete with a fin bearing the cinema's title. In the souvenir programme produced for the opening, the description read: 'The dominant feature on the building is the unique tower over the main entrance which has been equipped with neon lighting, and will form a local landmark for many miles, especially at night when alight'. Another unusual, though not unique feature (as it was employed in a number of earlier Odeons) was an upper tier of seats instead of a conventional circle or balcony. It did not overhang any of the downstairs stalls, and since it was lower than normal, gave the audience a more horizontal view of the screen. The raised tier, which was still referred to as the circle, seated 528, while the ground floor auditorium accommodated 989. The decoration throughout was in shades of old rose with speckled gold; all upholstery and carpeting were bright green; and several large chandeliers were suspended from a highly ornate ceiling. The screen was of a new all-metal variety, and the proscenium flanked by two large ornamental grilles in front of organ chambers which were superfluous since an organ was never installed in the theatre. But the stage included an extra large semicircular orchestra pit, with the front stalls being set further back then usual – an advantage for people in the cheaper seats. These were priced at 6d, 9d and 1s, and those in the circle 1s 6d and 2s.

Press announcements for the cinema's opening on Monday 19 December 1938, described the Ambassador as 'Hayes' most modern luxury theatre'. Perfectly true, but of course there was only one other – the five-year-old Corinth. The opening ceremony was performed by Colonel J.J. Llewellin, MP for Uxbridge, and attended by L.M. Graves JP, chairman of Hayes UDC, along with other councillors. The band of the 1st Battalion, The King's Own Scottish Borderers, was engaged to provide a musical interlude, as it had done six months earlier at the Uxbridge Odeon's opening. Coincidentally, the film chosen, *This Man is News*, featured the same star (Valerie Hobson) who had appeared at Uxbridge in June for the screening of *The Drum*. Miss Hobson had agreed to repeat her personal appearance with her fiancé Anthony Havelock-Allan, producer of the picture which was made at nearby Pinewood Studios. But unfortunately, she was prevented from attending through illness, and Mr Allan MacKinnon, co-writer of the screenplay took her place.

So now the residents of Hayes could enjoy 'first run' pictures for the first time – hitherto they had been obliged to travel further afield for the privilege. As a general rule the Ambassador ran exactly the same programmes as at Uxbridge and other Odeons. It could not have got off to a better start, for its first year of business, 1939, is generally considered as the greatest movie year of all time, apart from which, cinema admissions increased dramatically after the war started. However, one new patron, William K. Everson, said his enjoyment was tinged with guilt when he thought of his first love, the Regent, standing empty and unused across the road.

But another former Hayes resident, Don Mead, has nothing but the fondest memories of the 'Ambass'. And like Mr Everson, Don also remembered with affection his boyhood outings to the old Regent during the thirties. The Saturday morning serials made the greatest impact, but an extra thrill was being taken with his family one Saturday night to see his father marching through the town in a British Legion procession that featured in the newsreel.

In May 1941, at the age of fourteen, Don started work at the Ambassador as the eighth projectionist. His duties including making the tea, collecting cheese rolls for lunch, polishing floors, cleaning the chandeliers and, oh yes – learning to use the projectors by showing the newsreel. Don carried the newsreel three times a day to the newly built Savoy cinema on the Uxbridge Road, as it was shared by the two houses.

Newspaper advertisement for the opening of the Ambassador cinema in East Avenue, Hayes, at the end of 1938.

It was packed in a wooden box on the back of his bicycle, and on many journeys Don remembers stopping to collect pieces of shrapnel – remnants of anti-aircraft fire from the previous night's blitz – and he built up quite a collection. Don's working day began at 10 a.m. and ended at about 10.30 p.m. There were three breaks in between and he enjoyed one day off a week. Sunday hours were from 2.30 p.m. to 10.30 p.m. An hour before opening time, all staff went on an inspection parade in the main vestibule in accordance with the customary Odeon policy. The projectionists lined up in their white coats, and shoes had to be well polished. Projectors were cleaned every morning and the house chandeliers weekly. Part of Don's job on this exercise was to replace the glass dislodged during the anti-aircraft barrage of previous nights. Gramophone records (78s), chosen by Don, were played on the non-sync machine for 30 minutes after opening time before the programme began, and because their volume level was so consistent, the most-used were of Victor Sylvester's Dance Orchestra. Don's wartime memories of his spell at the Ambassador include watching the night sky lit up over London after a bombing raid, which could be seen from a flat roof adjacent to the projection box. He also recalls a thoughtful gesture made by the management to invite families who had seen any of their relatives on the newsreel, to a private showing during the following morning. Obviously they were servicemen and women, and Don recounted a particularly poignant morning when a family who lived in the same road as the cinema arrived to watch the newsreel in which they had seen their father a night or two before. Poignant because, before leaving the house, they received a telegram saying he had been killed in action.

But most of Don's recollections were of a happier nature – particularly some of the films he showed and special events staged by the cinema. In November 1941, a novel experiment involved devoting a whole week to Deanna Durbin films. So from Monday to Saturday, patrons enjoyed *Three Smart Girls*, *100 Men and a Girl*, *Mad About Music*, *That Certain Age*, *Three Smart Girls Grow Up*, and *First Love* – certainly a treat for Durbin fans. Other wartime events held at the Ambassador were 'Midnight Matinées', actually a misnomer, since they started at 10 p.m. and finished at 11.30! Proceeds for these shows, which featured many celebrated guest stars, went to the local Comforts Fund.

Don just couldn't keep away from the cinema, and even while in the Army he spent some of his leaves keeping his hand in by helping out the projectionists. After being demobbed he was back there showing *Hamlet* four times a day, including morning performances for hundreds of local schoolchildren. Then it was *Scott of the Antarctic* playing to packed houses and setting up a box office record which wasn't broken until 1961 with *The Magnificent Seven*. Another high spot was the visit of the London Philharmonic Orchestra on 1 February 1949. They gave two morning performances, each one being attended by 1,500 children. After the Regent's conversion to a theatre, many of the stars appearing there visited the Ambassador in the afternoon to relax before their evening show. Among them were Leo McKern, Terence Alexander and Diana Dors. Don recalled Diana being given tea in the staff room on one such occasion, and later that night a large packet of fish and chips was delivered to the projection room with a note: 'Thanks for the tea – DD'.

Frontage of the Ambassador showing the tower and fin, photographed during its opening week in December 1938, and advertising *This Man Is News* on the canopy.

According to newspaper accounts, the Rank Company's sudden decision to close the Ambassador came as a complete surprise, even to the manager. Apparently audience figures had not been falling, and the reason given for closure was that it 'was part of a general reorganization'. When the end came, on 10 June 1961, after the showing of *Nearly a Nasty Accident* and *Home is the Hero*, a local press headline announced 'the death of a cinema'. The once-proud building, now with its front entrance boarded up, looked shabby and forlorn as it stood idle for the next eight years, before being demolished to make way for a new GPO telephone exchange.

As for Don Mead, while the cinema went downhill, his career was on the ascent. After spending eleven years at the Rank Film Laboratories at Denham, where he met many celebrities including Charlie Chaplin, Elizabeth Bergner and her producer husband Paul Czinner, he became publicity manager of Sir Lew Grade's Incorporated Television Company (ITC). Not bad for the former fourteen-year-old tea boy!

The auditorium of the Ambassador, seen from the unusually low balcony, highlighting the ornate ceiling décor.

Another shot of the Ambassador interior, taken from the stalls.

The last picture of the Ambassador, taken during its closing week in 1961.

Memory Lane time for former Ambassador projectionist Don Mead, standing in front of the telephone exchange building that replaced the cinema where he spent many happy working hours.

Any glory that the owners of the Ambassador may have been basking in after opening the biggest and best cinema in Hayes lasted precisely fourteen days. For on 2 January 1939, the even bigger and better Savoy opened on the Uxbridge Road, just a mile away. It must have been an exciting prospect for the filmgoing public of Hayes, as they watched not one, but two new luxury cinemas springing up simultaneously.

The Savoy was the brainchild of the enterprising Glassman family, who, earlier in the decade, had opened another three Savoys at East Acton, Enfield and Burnt Oak. Prior to that, the family had interests in other East London picture houses during the late twenties. All their Savoy cinemas, including Hayes, were designed by renowned architect George Coles, probably best known for his work on many Odeon buildings. Clearing of the site began in April 1938, and various building problems arose from the outset. These were overcome, but progress was again severely disrupted during the Munich crisis in September by a labour shortage and a serious lack of materials. But despite all the difficulties, work was completed in time for the opening.

The cinema's impressive-looking frontage had a distinct advantage – being set well back from the main Uxbridge Road, to allow for an ample service area along the whole of the building. The *Kine Weekly* of 9 February 1939 described the frontage as: '...dignified, which due to its restraint and careful treatment, is suggestive of period architecture. The general rectangular shape is rendered very satisfying by the treatment of the centre portion incorporating the entrance. This is dominated by three finely proportioned windows with semicircular heads. Flanking and dividing these are four Corinthian columns in terracotta'. George Coles had certainly created a most imposing design – probably the best of any cinema for miles around. Most of the general facing was in buff brickwork, relieved by portions of faience tiling either side of the entrance and across the top of the pillars, where the name 'Savoy' stood out boldly. A final addition to the façade was a miniature balustrade along the top. Under the streamlined canopy which also bore the cinema's title, were three sets of double-entrance swing doors, divided by square faience-tiled pillars. Incoming patrons passing through the entrance vestibule into the main foyer must have been immediately impressed by the luxurious, almost palatial, effect of the fittings and decorations confronting them. Australian walnut panelling, concealed lighting troughs, pink and buff-coloured walls, cream ceilings, marble stairs and rich Wilton carpeting in red, green and beige – all combined to produce a feeling of opulence. Added furnishings included many colourful flower boxes, tall palms and a magnificent mirror above the landing of the stairway to the circle and café. It goes without saying that this eye-catching splendour spread throughout the rest of the interior: from the circle foyer and café to the auditorium whose total seating capacity was 2,200, made up of 1,400 in the stalls and 800 in the balcony (a total that exceeded that of any other house in the area). Dressing rooms and a large stage fitted with gold house tabs and a red pelmet had been installed, while a Compton organ mounted on a lift was the centrepiece of the orchestra pit.

All seats for the opening night had been sold in advance, and the full house had good value for money. The main feature was *Having Wonderful Time* with Ginger Rogers and Douglas Fairbanks Jnr, supported by *The Call of the Yukon*. In addition, a stage show was provided by a well-known comedian of the day, Leon Cortez, with his BBC Band of Coster Pals and Doreen Harris. Mr Lewis Glassman (son of the owner Abraham Glassman) acted as general manager of the Savoy, and spent most of his time looking after the cinema which was run by an under manager, Jimmy Christie. Now aged eighty-nine, Lewis (or Lew to his friends) still travels from London to visit friends in Hayes, and was pleased to reminisce about the Savoy's early days, when I met him recently. He told me that during the first few weeks of its existence, the cinema had been prevented from showing 'first run' releases. Apparently the proprietors of the Palace cinema in nearby Southall had been instrumental in having a ban imposed on the Savoy, because of its close proximity. Consequently, Lew was obliged to show films that were four or five months old – and this included the opening night presentation. Fortunately, the ban was lifted reasonably quickly, probably because the Savoy had secured contracts for exhibiting MGM and Warner Bros movies, whereas the Palace, being part of the Gaumont circuit, almost always screened other companies' product.

From its opening, the cinema staged variety acts as a backup to the films, and many big name stars appeared there throughout the years, including Max Miller (several times), Josephine Baker, Will Hay Jnr and his company, reprising his father's famous stage act *The Fourth Form at St Michael's*, and of course the Compton organ was a regular feature. The first organist to play at the Savoy was Norman Tilley, who later became a manager there. Lew told me that he booked the stage acts through variety agent Joe Collins (father of Joan), and that originally he had engaged Oscar Rabin and his band for the opening night. But the plans changed, and Leon Cortez and company took their place. However, another noted orchestra leader, Jack Payne, appeared with

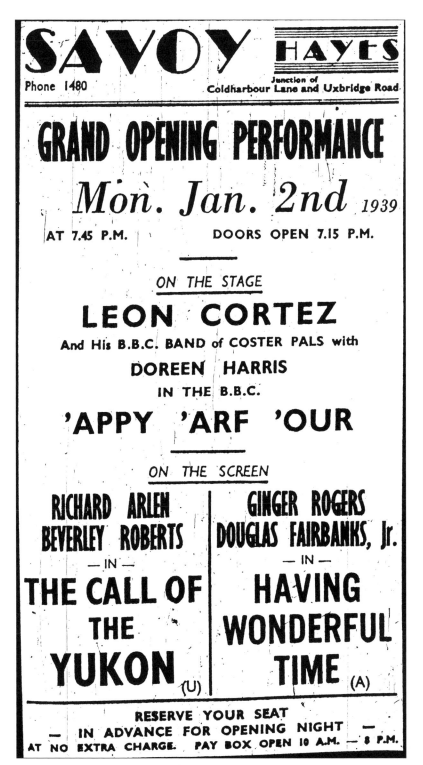

Newspaper advertisement for the opening of the Savoy, Hayes, in 1939.

his band and supporting artistes at an afternoon concert on Sunday 26 November 1940, presented by the Hayes War Entertainments Committee.

During the war, various 'spy' stories were circulating around Hayes – one suggesting that someone was signalling aircraft from the roof of the Savoy. Needless to say, the rumour was unfounded, but a light had been reported and Lew was summoned to appear at a local magistrates' court. Evidently, a projectionist had been opening his skylight window on hot summer nights, oblivious to the fact that flashes from the projector arc lamp were, periodically, lighting up the sky. But in court, the evidence provided was so conflicting that the magistrates quickly dismissed the case. Lew said it was the verdict he expected.

In the early 1940s, when the queues stretched round to the rear of the building, most of the Savoy's offerings did excellent business – among them *Rebecca*, *Blossoms in the Dust*, *Johnny Eager*, the Marx brothers in *Go West* and of course *Gone With the Wind*. But Lew was not entirely happy with the deal he had to accept when *GWTW* was booked for two consecutive weeks. Apart from having to increase admission prices (in common with all exhibitors), an extra percentage of gross takings claimed by the distributors resulted in the cinema's profit margin being lower than that for an average film.

During the fifties, the British Lion Film Corporation used the Savoy to present 'sneak previews' of their latest pictures. Occasionally the star of the film would make a personal appearance on stage, and one who Lew particularly remembered was William Hartnell. Another innovation at this time was the letting of the cinema on some Sunday afternoons for the showing of Indian films. Lew recalled that Indian residents of Southall dressed in their colourful 'Sunday best', flocked

Mr Abraham Glassman, cinema entrepreneur and owner of the Savoy.

Mr Lewis Glassman, who as general manager supervised the running of the Savoy for his father Abraham.

to the Savoy in their hundreds – and they brought their own films with them.

By the end of the decade, with cinema admissions in general on a downward spiral, the Glassman family decided to sell the Savoy, along with its namesake at Burnt Oak, to the Essoldo circuit. This company was about to close the Essoldo cinema (formerly the Corinth) further along the same road, and so after acquiring the Savoy, was able to operate it under its own name. On 14 October 1962, the Glassmans' old cinema reopened as the Essoldo, but after less than five years, was forced to close, on 3 September 1967. The last programme to be screened was *Goliath and the Vampires* and *Attack of the Crab Monsters*. A downmarket and gory end to a great cinema!

The Savoy's glory days were well remembered by Hayes resident Vera Baker. As a teenager, she patronized the cinema and others on a regular basis. Then, in 1954, she applied for a job there and became Lew Glassman's personal secretary, staying on after he left, until 1965. The days of crowds and queues were long gone; the café/restaurant was no more; and the biggest occasions that Vera could recall were a one-night show by Adam Faith and regular wrestling nights that were always a guaranteed sell-out.

After closure, Essoldo converted the auditorium into a bingo hall, eventually selling it to Ladbrokes who ran it as a social club. Currently, it operates under the name of Mecca Bingo. Inside the once-lavish vestibule is a battery of fruit and game machines, completely obscuring the grand staircase, which appears to be intact. Fortunately, at least certain parts of the building have a preservation order on them.

Hayes War Entertainments Committee

PRESENT

JACK PAYNE

AND HIS BAND

with Full Company of Supporting Artistes

— AT —

SAVOY CINEMA

UXBRIDGE ROAD, HAYES

at 2 p.m. on

SUNDAY, NOVEMBER 26th

NUMBERED RESERVED SEATS 2/6; RESERVED 2/-, 1/6, 1/-
ALL SEATS BOOKABLE
Box Office Now Open at Savoy Cinema.

Local newspaper advertisement, for a Sunday wartime concert at the Savoy, in 1940.

The magnificent frontage of the Savoy on the Uxbridge Road at Hayes, photographed prior to the opening.

The elegant staircase and walnut panelling in the vestibule of the Savoy, with the palms adding an exotic touch.

The Savoy's first floor circle foyer suggesting an ambience of luxurious comfort.

A side view of the Savoy auditorium showing the Compton organ at the top of its lift and the ashtrays attached to every other seat.

A view from the Savoy balcony giving a palatial effect.

The interior of the borough's largest cinema, pictured from the stage where many variety acts took place.

The Savoy's original general manager Mr Lewis Glassman during a recent visit to Hayes.

After the Essoldo closed in 1967, Hayes was left without a cinema for almost five years. When a new one finally emerged, it was located, somewhat surprisingly, immediately next-door. Named the 'Classic', it was the latest addition to the long-standing Classic chain of cinemas. To say that the building resembled a narrow, oblong box would not be an unfair description. Certainly it bore no resemblance to a conventional cinema, and perched as it was on top of a supermarket, it could in fact have been anything. Furthermore, since part of it was joined to the adjacent Essoldo, it stood out like the proverbial sore thumb. However, the Classic Group's publicity director declared that no effort had been spared to create an intimate atmosphere inside the auditorium, and to provide the utmost comfort for patrons. He was referring to orange curtains hanging all around the interior walls, plush carpeting and extra comfortable seats with plenty of legroom. The auditorium, which accommodated 400, was approached through a very small main entrance and foyer. But the Classic did boast the latest sound and projection equipment, and its main projector had an automatic rewind facility, capable of carrying 13,000ft of film on a single reel – enough to accommodate a full programme. It was the only one of its type in London, and there were only another two sets in the UK.

The Classic's policy was to show what it considered to be the best of the general releases, with particular emphasis on films not making the rounds of established circuits. Children's Saturday morning pictures were introduced from the outset – also a 'Late Movie Show' on Saturday nights starting at 11 p.m., which featured a different programme from the rest of the week. Later a 'Family Matinée' programme for parents and children was presented on Saturday afternoons.

The Classic, described in the advertisements as an 'Exciting New Cinema', opened on the afternoon of Friday 2 June 1972, with Ken Russell's film version of *The Boy Friend* starring Twiggy. Being the only cinema in Hayes, it met with considerable success in its early days, with films like *Night of the Generals*, *Bob and Carol and Ted and Alice* and Brando's *The Wild One* – the last two being X-rated. A *Clockwork Orange* together with *Kama Sutra Rides Again* were held over for a second week 'owing to enormous success' according to newspaper advertisements. But it was made clear that neither of these pictures would be shown at the Saturday Family Matinée!

During the 1980s the little cinema experienced what so many others had done previously – a big drop in patronage – despite having the distinction of being the only surviving picture house in the whole of the borough for the last three and a half years of its existence. But it did not go down without a fight. The staff organized a last-minute petition signed by 15,000 residents, which failed to dissuade the cinema's parent company, Cannon, from withdrawing its decision to close. The directors declared that it was no longer profitable, and that as a single screen cinema, it had been losing an economic battle with the multiplexes. So the Classic screened its final film, *Back to the Future*, to a full house on 2 January 1986. At the time of writing, the building is still in place with all the shops beneath it boarded up and plastered with posters advertising 'Bollywood' films

EXCITING NEW CINEMA
classic
UXBRIDGE ROAD *(Adjoining Essoldo)* Tel. 848 8401

OPENS THIS FRIDAY JUNE 2nd
THE FINEST MOVIE ENTERTAINMENT IN LUXURIOUS SURROUNDINGS AND CARPETED COMFORT!

FABULOUS OPENING PRESENTATION

TWIGGY in KEN RUSSELL'S film of
THE BOY FRIEND U

Continuous Programmes 3.00 5.30 8.00

Newspaper advertisement for the opening of the Classic cinema, Uxbridge Road, Hayes, in 1972.

and pop concerts, while next door, the bingo hall presumably continues to enjoy a thriving trade.

Five years after the opening of the Classic, a new council-built theatre was erected in Grange Road, just a short distance away. Starting life as the Alfred Beck Centre, then renamed the Beck Theatre, its prime function was to present stage productions. But it was also fully equipped as a cinema, with a seating capacity of 600, arranged in stadium style. Since its opening in 1977, the Beck has continued to show a small number of films each year, usually for one night only, as they have to be programmed between the stage shows which are booked a year in advance. The theatre thus provides a service, albeit a limited one, to the people of Hayes who can at least still claim to have one big screen left in the town.

A recent picture of the now-defunct Classic, with a row of shops beneath it – also closed. Its proximity to the Essoldo (formerly Savoy) highlights the marked difference in architectural styles between the 1930s and the 1970s.

Three

Northwood, Eastcote and Ruislip: From Picture Theatre to Dining Club

The rural community of Northwood was the first in the district to enjoy silent movies at a newly-built cinema. One year after another Londoner, Jack Hutton, had moved to Uxbridge and opened his first cinema there, Maude and Bert Pope from Brixton Hill arrived in Northwood in 1911 with their family in a horse-drawn van. They moved into a house in Half-Mile Lane, later renamed High Street, and supervised the building of the 425-seater picture house opposite, for the owner, Mr Lill. Bert had been the commissionaire of the New Royalty cinema in Brixton, and when the new Northwood Picture Theatre opened in 1913, he became its first manager. His family made a big contribution to the running of the cinema. His wife Maude operated the pay box and acted as an usherette, his sister Winnie Sadler was the pianist, and his brother-in-law Percy Sadler doubled as the commissionaire and sound effects man – his props consisted of a bass drum and coconut shells. The only non-family member of staff was George Dale, the projectionist.

Life in the cinema was soon disrupted by the outbreak of the First World War in 1914. Bert enlisted in the Army in 1915 along with his brother-in-law, and projectionist George Dale followed shortly afterwards, which left Maude Pope to run the picture house almost single-handedly. George had taught her how to run and rewind the films (manually, of course) and her sons Horace and Len carried them to and from Northwood station on a cart. The Picture Theatre was extremely popular throughout the war – not only with the locals for whom the new medium of moving pictures was an exciting novelty, but also with the soldiers billeted in the village, who had special shows put on for them. Programmes included Charlie Chaplin shorts, the ever popular *Quo Vadis*, newsreels featuring British victories in the war, and the inevitable serials. After the war, business started to slump and the Popes had to resort to letting out the building three times a week for parties. Finally they severed their connection with the picture house in 1919, and started a decorating business.

The Northwood Picture House shortly after its opening in 1913. Staff (from left to right) are Percy Sadler, commissionaire and sound effects man; George Dale, projectionist; Maude Pope, the manager's wife; Winnie Sadler, pianist; and the manager Albert Pope.

The cinema then appeared to go through a period of constant name changes in the space of two years, probably due to frequent changes of ownership. After the Popes' departure, it was renamed Ritz, then Northwood Cinema, then Playhouse in May 1921, when the new proprietors were listed as Stanley Cinemas Ltd. The directors, J.W.G. and H.O. Stanley, introduced several innovations including programme changes every Monday and Thursday, matinées on Wednesdays and Saturdays, and an orchestra at all performances. They also advertised *Pathé Gazette* newsreels and the magazine programmes *Pathé Pictorial* and *Pathé Sunbeams* as accompanying features. By April 1932, local newspaper advertisements included the name of a new manager and proprietor, Alfred Dove, while in July 1934, the cinema itself underwent its final name change, and became the Tatler, under entirely new management. Unfortunately, its days were numbered, as after two years, plans were announced for a large, luxury cinema just around the corner, with which it could not have competed. Six years on, in 1942, the building was converted to a wartime British Restaurant, and then in 1954 it was purchased by the local council. Originally used for offices, it now serves as a dining club for the Ruislip and Northwood Old Folks' Association, looking very much like it did as the Picture Theatre in 1913.

The Picture House in 1914 just after the outbreak of the First World War. Recruitment posters are much in evidence, together with a notice inviting the public to donate cigarettes for wounded soldiers.

Half-Mile Lane, Northwood (later renamed High Street), showing the Picture House sandwiched between a row of terraced houses.

PLAY HOUSE NORTHWOOD

Programme for November.

NOW SHOWING—
THE EVER OPEN DOOR, by Geo. R. Sims.

Monday, November 7th.　　　For 3 Days only.

MARY PICKFORD
—IN—
MADAME BUTTERFLY
Matinee, Wednesday 3 p.m.

Thursday, **THE HOUND OF THE BASKERVILLES,**
Nov. 10th.　By Sir Arthur Conan Doyle.

Monday, **BLEAK HOUSE,**
Nov. 14th.　By Charles Dickens.

Thursday, **GERALDINE FARRAR,**
Nov. 17th.　In THE WOMAN AND THE PUPPET.

Monday, **WILLIAM FARNUM,**
Nov. 21st.　In THE ADVENTURER.

Thursday, **CONSTANCE TALMADGE,**
Nov. 24th.　In THE PERFECT WOMAN.

Monday, Nov. 28th.　　　For 3 Days only.

LITTLE DORRIT
BY CHARLES DICKENS.
Matinee, Wednesday, 3 p.m.

ORCHESTRA AT ALL PERFORMANCES

Continuous Performance from 6.15 p.m.
Matinees, Saturdays, at 3 p.m.

Proprietors:—STANLEY CINEMAS LTD.
Directors: J. W. G. STANLEY and H. O. STANLEY.

A 1921 newspaper advertisement for the cinema, now renamed the Playhouse.

Yet another new name as the Northwood cinema is now advertised as the Tatler in a 1935 newspaper.

A recent picture of the cinema building, now serving as a dining club for senior citizens.

This side view of the Northwood Dining Club indicates that nothing much has changed since it was built in 1911 as the Picture Theatre. Modern cars look out of place.

Just a couple of miles away from the Northwood Playhouse, in the sleepy village of Eastcote, the next cinema to appear on the local scene was the quaint little Ideal. The proprietors were Telling Bros Ltd (later W.A. Telling Ltd), prominent builders in the area. During 1924 to 1926, they built a dignified-looking parade of shops complete with two-storey flats, along Eastcote's main street, Field End Road. A year later, they decided to add a multipurpose community hall at the end of the parade, designed to blend in perfectly with the adjacent terraced buildings with their Swiss chalet-style roofs and tall gable ends. It was named, appropriately, Field End Hall. With new housing developments springing up all over 'Metro-land' (a vast area covered by the extended Metropolitan railway), the Tellings had obviously felt that the rapidly rising population of Eastcote and its environs would need a new entertainment venue.

Mr Telling, a local benefactor and a great patron of the dramatic arts, opened his new hall on Saturday 10 December 1927 with a dance, and engaged a London Dance Band for the occasion. Subsequently, he advertised 'Dancing Every Wednesday' with cabaret and carnival dances at weekends. In 1928, a production of *The Gondoliers* was the first stage show to be presented and this was followed by the Pinner and Harrow Musical Society performing *The Geisha*. A local press report described the hall as 'one of the best in the district for theatrical performances and in this case, operas'. But after only a year, it was evident that dances and shows were not the viable proposition envisaged by the owners. So they changed direction, converted the building into a cinema, and christened it the Ideal – a name they used for their large, detached houses.

The opening film, on Thursday 3 January 1929, was a silent version of Zane Grey's *Under the Tonto Rim* featuring Richard Arlen and Mary Brian. It was supported by a comedy, *My Friend From India*, plus the newsreel, and advertised as a 'Special Attraction' with the added incentive that patrons' return rail fares would be reimbursed on production of their tickets at the pay box. Another item included in the advertisement stated that the Ideal was two minutes from Eastcote station, whereas

Newspaper advertisement for the opening of the Ideal cinema, Eastcote, in 1929.

The Ideal, Eastcote, c. 1937.

previous advertisements for the Field End Hall had quoted one minute. A fortnight later, it had extended to three minutes. Soon afterwards, it was omitted altogether! For the first few years, there was only one programme a week, running from Thursday to Saturday, and then only in the evenings. But a children's Saturday matinée was introduced from 20 January 1929. Admission prices were 6d, 9d, 1s, 1s 6d and 2s.

In 1933, new and up-to-date BTH sound apparatus was installed, and patrons could enjoy a change of programme every Monday and Thursday, plus matinées on Wednesdays and Saturdays. By now the Ideal's newspaper advertisements took the form of a three-pronged notice under a general heading that read: 'Eastcote Offers the Following Facilities to Visitors and Residents.' Then came the week's film programme, with an advertisement for Ideal Motors and Garage underneath, followed by one for the Manor House hotel. The garage and the public house were the cinema's next-door neighbours and the picture house and motor company shared the same telephone number. As this was also the number of Telling's Estate Office in Eastcote station, some callers may have been confused!

Films booked at the Ideal were invariably several months old, but were always interesting 'big' pictures, even if some of the prints were less than perfect. After Sunday opening was legalized, still older pictures were shown, and at least that meant six old movies per week – useful to film fans who had missed them earlier.

When cinemas reopened after the brief shutdown at the start of the Second World War, the Ideal had an outsize tarpaulin erected around the entrance to act as a light trap during the blackout. But by 1941, a more sophisticated method was used. Performances were rescheduled to end earlier (at 10 p.m.) and during 1940, members of the Methodist congregation held some of their services there – a multipurpose hall still!

Cinema-going at the Ideal was quite a unique experience. There was no entrance foyer, the pay box was almost on the pavement, and the door to the auditorium, which seated 412, was only a step away. The sound of traffic outside could be heard when the door was opened, and patrons sitting in back rows could hear people paying at the desk. Space was at a premium; seating was all on one level, and very basic; the whole set up was reminiscent of 'the Smallest Show on Earth'. One very rarely saw an usherette and the manager at the time (in the early forties) doubled as an odd-job man – sometimes in the pay box, occasionally selling ice creams – and could quite frequently be seen carrying a long ladder, upright, across the front of the screen, on his way to do some running repairs. His versatility also extended to tearing tickets and showing customers to their seats.

During this period I was a frequent visitor to the Ideal: not to sample the delights of the décor, which, quite honestly, was non-existent, but because from the time when the cinema was equipped with sound (its initial offering was Warner Bros' *I Am a Fugitive From a Chain Gang*), it seemed to book that company's pictures more than any other. Since they were my particular favourites, I spent many happy hours there in the 1940s. As most of them carried an A certificate, I had been too young to see them first time round.

The Ideal was, not surprisingly, the first cinema casualty in the area, with the exception of the Northwood Tatler, twenty years earlier. It closed on 30 May 1956, with *The Far Horizons* and *Triple Blackmail*, and was redeveloped into a garage by Ideal Motors whose name at least perpetuated the cinema's identity, but only until the garage itself was demolished to make way for an office block.

Eastcote residents may have considered the Ideal as unfashionable, and understandably so when comparing it with much grander picture houses in neighbouring areas such as Harrow, Pinner and Rayners Lane. But it had provided cinematic entertainment for twenty-seven years and, for me anyway, had a certain cosy charm all of its own. And I still spare a thought for that hard-working manager – surely he was the stuff that the old-time cinema showmen

Field End Road, Eastcote, resplendent with Coronation decorations in May 1937. The Ideal cinema is in the centre of the picture; in Coronation week it played host to crippled children from nearby St Vincent's Hospital by presenting a special film show for them.

were made of.

Just nine months after the opening of the Ideal came the arrival of the first cinema in the leafy garden suburb of Ruislip. It was advertised in the local press as 'The New Cinema – Rivoli, Ruislip', and opened on Monday 30 September 1929 with the film *Champagne*, starring Betty Balfour. The event was greeted with great enthusiasm by the populace who turned out in large numbers to celebrate the occasion. The cinema was conveniently situated for Ruislip residents, with its location in Ickenham Road, just a few yards off the High Street. In addition, the Metropolitan railway station was within walking distance. Described by the press as 'having a dignified façade in the Grecian style', the Rivoli was designed by architect F.C. Mitchell, who, nine years later, would be responsible for the Hayes Ambassador. The square frontage was plain and unpretentious, but nevertheless had a certain elegance. Set well back from the road, with an extra-wide pavement in front of its entrance steps, plus plenty of access space on both sides of the building, it assumed an air of greater importance than its size might suggest. A relatively small house with a seating capacity of 757, it was still big enough to include a balcony, a modest foyer, a tea lounge and a stage for variety shows. More importantly it was equipped for the new invention – 'talkies' – although 'silents' were still shown in the early days. The seats in the auditorium were of the tip-up type – and 'bucket type' in the balcony – all upholstered in a luxurious shade of blue.

Programmes were changed on Mondays and Thursdays (initially only evening performances), with matinées on Wednesdays and Saturdays. Admission prices were 6d, 1s, 1s 3d, 1s 10d and 2s 4d. Sound films were introduced in the early 1930s and although the stage does not appear to have been used for professional shows, the Ruislip Operatic Society performed there at various times during the decade. For a week in October 1937, films took a back seat when the company presented *The Vagabond King*. No provision had been made for dressing rooms backstage, and the society was obliged to erect marquees in the car park for this purpose. In 1934, Mr Charles F. Cheshir became the proprietor of the Rivoli – previously he had owned the Playhouse at Gerrards Cross. But by 1936, the cinema was acquired by the small but up-and-coming circuit, Shipman and King. The company, who advertised themselves as 'S&K', had built up a chain of houses in Surrey, Kent, Hampshire, Buckinghamshire and Cambridgeshire, and others would follow. Soon afterwards the policy of changing the programme in mid-week was phased out, and continuous performances ran from Monday to Saturday in line with the other major cinemas.

After screening its last film, *Moment to Moment*, with Honor Blackman, and *The Ghost and Mr Chicken*, the Rivoli closed on 4 June 1966. A Sainsbury's supermarket was built in its place, itself now demolished in favour of an apartment block.

It was probably inevitable in a rapidly expanding community like Ruislip, which stretched to West and South Ruislip and Ruislip Manor, that a second cinema would follow the birth of the Rivoli. However, it was a full five years before it materialized, during which time the Rivoli enjoyed a monopoly. The new arrival, named the Astoria, occupied a commanding position in the High Street, virtually in the centre of the town, and even nearer to the railway station than its rival. Not that rivalry was a factor, because with a glut of pictures available, there was ample scope for two houses in a town with Ruislip's population.

```
THE NEW CINEMA.
RIVOLI, RUISLIP
          —Near Met. Station.

Continuous Performance from 6.15.    Matinee : Wed. & Sat., 2.30.

MONDAY NEXT, SEPTEMBER 30th.    For Three Days.

Betty Balfour in CHAMPAGNE
    Also  Comedy—Interest  and  Super  Gazette.

THURSDAY, OCTOBER 3rd.    For Three Days.

Mabel Poulton in NOT QUITE A LADY
    Also. Comedy—Novelty  and  Super  Gazette.

Prices :  6d.,   1/-,   1/3,   1/10,   &   2/4 (Including Tax).
```

Local press advertisement for the opening of the Rivoli, Ruislip, in 1929.

The Astoria, which seated over 900, was designed by distinguished architect J. Stanley Beard, who was responsible for many cinemas in and around London during the thirties, including the Forum, Ealing. Mr Beard's work on the external elevation was in the then-modern style, with multicoloured brickwork and white rendering on the frontage, which was dominated by three arch-shaped windows above the canopy. A short flight of steps led up to the front entrance, where four sets of doors were flanked by quite wide expanses on either side, for billboards and showcases. Inside, the foyer was noticeably small, with just enough room for a pay box, kiosk and staircase to the upstairs balcony. Interior decoration consisted of warm beige tints with green and gold trimmings.

Mr Charles Cheshir, who had just taken over the running of the Rivoli, became the Astoria's first proprietor with the assistance of his son Eric. In the press announcement of the opening on Monday 24 September 1934, he described his latest enterprise as 'The Cinema Supreme', and engaged stage and film star Hugh Wakefield to perform the opening ceremony. The film chosen was Catherine the Great with Elizabeth Bergner and Douglas Fairbanks Jnr, supported by a Laurel and Hardy short and a Walt Disney cartoon. Large crowds had gathered long before the doors opened, and they filled the downstairs auditorium, while the invited guests occupied the circle seats. Before the speeches began, an orchestra provided some additional entertainment. As with almost all other houses, the Astoria changed its programmes on Mondays and Thursdays. Like the others, afternoon shows were confined to Wednesdays and Saturdays. Admission charges were 9d, 1s, 1s 6d. 1s 10d and 2s 6d.

The Rivoli, Ruislip, soon after its opening.

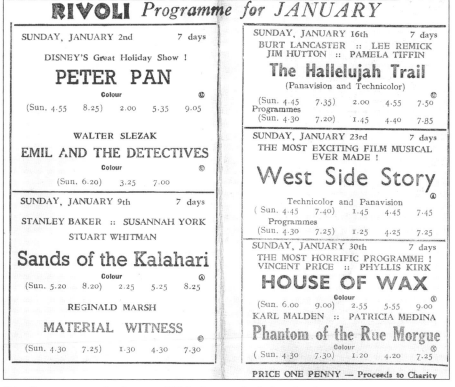

RIVOLI *Programme for* JANUARY

SUNDAY, JANUARY 2nd   7 days

DISNEY'S Great Holiday Show !

PETER PAN
Colour

(Sun. 4.55   8.25)   2.00   5.35   9.05

WALTER SLEZAK

EMIL AND THE DETECTIVES
Colour

(Sun. 6.20)   3.25   7.00

SUNDAY, JANUARY 9th   7 days

STANLEY BAKER :: SUSANNAH YORK
STUART WHITMAN

Sands of the Kalahari
Colour

(Sun. 5.20   8.20)   2.25   5.25   8.25

REGINALD MARSH

MATERIAL WITNESS

(Sun. 4.30   7.25)   1.30   4.30   7.30

SUNDAY, JANUARY 16th   7 days
BURT LANCASTER :: LEE REMICK
JIM HUTTON :: PAMELA TIFFIN

The Hallelujah Trail
(Panavision and Technicolor)

(Sun. 4.45   7.35)   2.00   4.55   7.50
Programmes
(Sun. 4.30   7.20)   1.45   4.40   7.85

SUNDAY, JANUARY 23rd   7 days
THE MOST EXCITING FILM MUSICAL
EVER MADE !

West Side Story

Technicolor and Panavision
(Sun. 4.45   7.40)   1.45   4.45   7.45
Programmes
(Sun. 4.30   7.25)   1.25   4.25   7.25

SUNDAY, JANUARY 30th   7 days
THE MOST HORRIFIC PROGRAMME !
VINCENT PRICE :: PHYLLIS KIRK

HOUSE OF WAX
Colour

(Sun. 6.00   9.00)   2.55   5.55   9.00
KARL MALDEN :: PATRICIA MEDINA

Phantom of the Rue Morgue
Colour

(Sun. 4.30   7.30)   1.20   4.20   7.25

PRICE ONE PENNY — Proceeds to Charity

The Rivoli programme for January 1966, six months before its closure.

The Ruislip Rivoli in 1965.

Another view of the Ruislip Rivoli taken during the sixties.

Five months later, in February 1935, a Jessie Matthews picture, *The Midshipmaid*, was screened by special request and *The Last Gentleman* starring George Arliss occupied the second half of the week. Both programmes were featured in the same press advertisement, and represented quite a coincidence as the two leading artistes had local connections. Jessie Matthews, an international celebrity, lived in Ruislip for some time, and her ashes are buried in St Martin's cemetery on the opposite side of the road to the Astoria, while Academy Award winner George Arliss lived periodically in Harrow Weald a few miles away, where his parents and sister also had houses. It was here that he was married, and is now buried, close to his parents in the All Saints' church part of Harrow Weald cemetery.

By 1936, the Astoria, together with the Rivoli, had become part of the Shipman and King circuit. The new owners now applied to the Ruislip UDC for permission to open their cinemas on Sundays. Although the bill to legalize Sunday opening had been given a second reading as far back as April 1931, it was a further three years (or more in some districts) before being finally approved by local councils. Uxbridge, Hayes and West Drayton councils had sanctioned Sunday opening in 1933-34, but only after long drawn-out debates. Although it was now five years since the bill had been passed, the people of Ruislip, Northwood and Eastcote were unable to go to the pictures on a Sunday. At least not in their own towns – and they still couldn't after the meeting between Shipman and King and Ruislip UDC, which the press labelled as 'a fiasco'. Only 103 people attended out of a total population of 36,000; the vote was decided by a show of hands; and the application rejected by eighty-two to twenty-one.

However in June 1937, Shipman and King, undeterred by their defeat, made a further application, and this time the whole procedure was conducted on similar lines to a general election. Polling day was on Saturday 19 June, and the booths were open for twelve hours. On the previous day, placarded cars with loudspeakers toured the district, while both sides in the debate issued manifestos to every household. On voting day, the cinema trade provided a fleet of thirty or forty cars to transport people to the polling stations, one vehicle being driven by well-known BBC singer Stuart Robertson, who had offered his services to aid the cause. But in spite of all the propaganda from the opposing factions, only twenty-eight per cent of the electorate bothered to vote, resulting in a victory for the cinema owners by the narrow majority of 541 – a result that was greeted with great delight by the victors, despite the apparent apathy on the part of the residents.

And so on Sunday 5 September 1937, both the Astoria and Rivoli opened their doors on the Sabbath for the first time, and the Ideal soon followed suit. The film selected by the Astoria was *Desire*, with Dietrich and Gary Cooper – a title that might not have gone down too well with the anti-opening lobby!

Meanwhile, in August, plans had been drawn up and artists' impressions published in the press of two new cinemas in the area. Both were to be part of the small Grosvenor circuit, which had recently opened a splendid house in Rayners Lane. The two proposed sites were in Field End Road, Eastcote (despite the presence of the Ideal)

ASTORIA

The

CHARLES F. CHESHIR

THE OPENING CEREM

WILL

MONDAY, SEPTEM

(THENCE NIGHTY AT 8.45 P.M. —

When it will be formally opened

Mr. HUGH

AFTER WHI

CATHERINE

ELIZABETH BERGNER &

AND A SPECIAL

THURSDAY, SEPTEMBER 27th.   3 NIG

FLYING DOWN TO RIO

TOO BEAUTIFUL FOR WOF

PRICES OF ADMISSION: STALLS 9d., 1/-, 1/6, 1/10; BA

Newspaper advertisement for the official opening of the Astoria in 1934.

Cinema
eme

RUISLIP

TELEPHONE—RUISLIP 2960

Y OF THIS THEATRE

ACE ON

R 24th, at 8 p.m.

TUESDAY & WEDNESDAY AT 2.30 P.M.)

Celebrated Stage and Film Star,

WAKEFIELD

E SCREENED

THE GREAT

OUGLAS FAIRBANKS Jnr.

RTING PROGRAMME

MATINEES SATURDAY, AT 2.30 P.M.

Dolores Del Rio & Fred Astaire

THEY SET IT TO MUSIC!

1/10, 2/6.   MATINEES: REDUCED PRICES.

and on the corner of Pembroke and Victoria Roads at Ruislip Manor. But as in the case of the proposed Hillingdon 'Gloria', although plans had seemingly been approved, neither project materialized. Many years later in the 1950s, a second attempt was made to obtain approval for a picture house on the Ruislip Manor corner site. Presumably, permission was refused, as a branch of Woolworth's was built instead. On this occasion, the applicants were the giant ABC group, who consoled themselves some years later when they acquired the Astoria in 1967. The thirty-three-year-old building was then subjected to a complete refurbishment programme. Seating capacity was reduced to 800, giving patrons extra comfort; the frontage given an entirely new look; and the cinema renamed 'Embassy'. But when the scaffolding was removed, revealing the new frontage, traditionalists may well have thought that the facelift was hardly an improvement. The original simple but elegant design of the façade, including its three large windows, had been completely obliterated and replaced with a nondescript, futuristic-looking surround.

The cinema reopened on 30 April 1967, and because of the closure of its neighbour, the Rivoli, a year earlier, was then the only one in the town. It prospered for over fourteen years, but was forced to close on 28 November 1981 after its last presentation of *10* and *Private Benjamin*. The building stood empty for three years before being demolished, and the site was redeveloped as a block of shops and offices.

Most of the pre-war generation tend to indulge in periodic trips down Memory Lane, but what about this for a slice of real nostalgia: during the demolition, a Ruislip man who had patronized the Astoria regularly for thirty years retrieved an armrest and a piece of plaster coving as relics of an era that will never return.

The large, luxury cinema that was destined to spring up just around the corner from

The last picture of the Rivoli in June 1966, advertising its last picture, *Moment to Moment*.

The frontage of the Ruislip Astoria, photographed soon after its opening.

Elizabeth Bergner and Douglas Fairbanks Jnr in *Catherine the Great*, the opening film at the Astoria. The Fairbanks family often featured in opening films at our local cinemas. Douglas Jnr starred in *Having Wonderful Time* at the Savoy, Hayes, in 1939, and his father appeared in *Reaching For The Moon*, the Uxbridge Regal's first film in 1931.

Press advertisement for the Astoria in February, 1935. Both main films during the week featured artistes with local connections. Jessie Matthews lived in Ruislip for some time, and her ashes are buried in the churchyard near the cinema. George Arliss lived for part of his life in nearby Harrow, and is buried here.

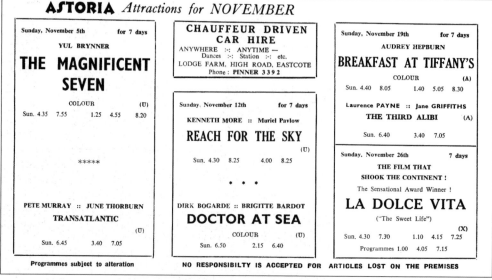

The Astoria programme for November 1961.

The commemorative wall plaque for Jessie Margaret Matthews in a dark corner of St Martin's cemetery in Ruislip High Street. The epitaph includes a quotation from Ecclesiastes – 'A time to live and a time to die'. A rosebush was planted nearby and named after her.

The Ruislip Astoria in 1964.

The Astoria undergoing refurbishment in 1967, with its name in the process of elimination.

A new-style programme dated May 1969 for the former Astoria – now renamed the Embassy.

A 1977 picture of the Embassy, illustrating the complete transformation of the original Astoria façade.

the Northwood Tatler, and which led, indirectly, to its demise, was the Rex in Pinner Road. Early in 1936, Odeon chief Oscar Deutsch had engaged architect Andrew Mather to design another addition to his steadily growing circuit, in the form of a 1,000-seater cinema at Northwood Hills. Two years later, Mather was re-engaged to plan the Uxbridge Odeon. But after completion of the Northwood building, the proposed opening date of September 1936 was delayed and in mid-November it was sold off to the Ruislip cinema owners, Shipman and King, whose circuit opened and operated it until closure. The owners, who now ran a trio of houses in the same catchment area, opened their latest acquisition on Monday 28 December 1936 – the original name 'Odeon' having been removed from the frontage and replaced by its new title Rex – a name that looked out of place on the façade of a typical Odeon building. It had been built by Harry Neal Ltd, a renowned firm of local contractors, who, in 1937, created Britain's largest cinema, the 4,004-seater Gaumont State at Kilburn. Andrew Mather's design for the front elevation, using very large faience tiling, gave the building an impressive appearance. The tiles created an illusion of extra width across the frontage which was set well back from the main road, with a small access area in front of the entrance, and this vast expanse of tiling was relieved by a number of neatly shaped windows above and at either side of the canopy. The interior was described in the local press as follows:

'The whole of the auditorium commands instant admiration for its sense of quiet magnificence, dignity and luxury. The long overdone gaudy grandiloquence of modern film palaces is missing – completely eclipsed by the restful treatment of walls and ceiling in the quietest pastel shades, effected with a maximum of colour.'

The report went on to extol the virtues of the 'expensive ventilating system; the

The Odeon building at Northwood Hills, photographed immediately after completion in 1936. Originally built for the Odeon chain, it was sold to the Shipman and King circuit before opening in December 1936 under the name Rex.

Charles of STATION PARADE

"HAIR STYLING WITH YOU IN MIND"

Fully Qualified Staff

Phone **NORTHWOOD** 25980

Sunday, July 29th   7 days

ELVIS PRESLEY

Follow That Dream

Colour   (U)

(Sun 4.30   7.55)   1.40   5.10   8.30

DON BEDDOE :: ELLEN CORBY

SAINTLY SINNERS

(U)

(Sun. 6.30)   3.40   7.00

FOR A FINE SELECTION OF GREETING CARDS
FOR **ALL** OCCASIONS

M. F. HIGSON

BOOKSELLER -::- **STATIONER**

22 HIGH ST.   Tel. : Northwood 3484

PRICE ONE PENNY

S&K

REX NORTHWOOD HILLS   Phone : 21644

CONTINUOUS DAILY

from 1.30 p.m.
Doors open 1.15 p.m.

Sundays from 4.30 p.m.
Doors open 4.15 p.m.

****

ATTRACTIONS FOR

● **JULY**

****

PRICES :
Stalls 2/6 3/6 ; Circle 4/3

LARGE FREE CAR PARK

FREE DEAF AIDS

★A **SHIPMAN & KING THEATRE**

The Rex, Northwood Hills, programme for July 1962.

delicately curved stage; and the double sets of shimmering silk curtains extending majestically almost up to the lofty ceiling'. A clear case of waxing lyrical!

The Rex was officially opened by Lieutenant-Commander S.W. Todd. Local District Councillors with their wives occupied two rows in the balcony. The opening programme featured Ralph Lynn and Claude Dampier in *All In*, together with *Border Flight* and a Disney cartoon. During its first year, the cinema's policy was to change the programme in mid-week; then through 1938 and 1939, it was varied so that certain films ran for six days; after which the only change was on Sundays. Seat prices ranged from 6d, 9d and 1s to 1s 6d and 2s, but a special attraction for matinee patrons was the offer of 800 seats at sixpence and over 200 at a shilling.

During the Sunday opening campaign of June 1937, two well-known actors lent their support on the Friday before polling day. They were Billy Milton and Hugh Wakefield, who had formally opened the Astoria in 1934, Both men addressed the evening audience at the Rex, urging them to vote, and they repeated their stint on the stage of the Ruislip Rivoli. When the result was declared on the following night, the Rex was chosen as the venue for celebrations by representatives of the cinema industry. The gentlemen concerned, armed with a goodly supply of fireworks, went up on to the roof of the cinema and organized their own display.

The Rex in 1968.

But apparently, one of the firecrackers fell into the road below, and – enter a local bobby – there was a premature end to the celebrations!

After that, the cinema led an uneventful existence as it continued to serve quite a wide area, until closing on 22 September 1973 with the Bond film *Live and Let Die*. In common with the Rivoli, the Rex's life had lasted thirty-seven years. And also, like the Rivoli, it was replaced by a supermarket after demolition.

No record of the cinemas in the Ruislip area would be complete without reference to a contribution by the Compass Theatre in Ickenham. Essentially an arts theatre for drama and music, it presented several seasons of silent movies during the seventies and eighties, when under the direction of John Sherratt. The films were accompanied by the celebrated pianist Florence de Jong, a musical director of the National Film Theatre. Florence, whom I was privileged to meet on many occasions, played at the theatre for over ten years, by which time she was well into her eighties. When she was finally forced to retire, her slightly younger sister Ena Baga, herself a well-known organist and pianist, took over. Today the Compass operates solely as a theatre.

Demolition of the thirty-seven-year-old Rex is almost complete.

Four

Yiewsley and West Drayton: From Serials to Supermarkets

Although Uxbridge had the distinction of being the first town in the borough to establish a purpose-built cinema, its near neighbours Yiewsley and West Drayton came a close second. For just five months after the birth of Rockingham Hall, the first picture house in Yiewsley opened in early 1911.

Plans for the conversion of an existing building in Station Road – a continuation of Yiewsley High Street – were approved on 3 December 1910, and work began a fortnight later. The new hall was the brainchild of three enterprising businessmen from Eton Wick – Messrs Hobbs, Smith and Pocock, who named it the Peoples' Electric Theatre. Building contractors from the same area, Burfoot and Son, completed the conversion in the surprisingly short time of six weeks, including the Christmas holiday period, and the cinema opened on 28 January 1911.

The building was a simple, oblong construction measuring 60ft by 35ft, with an engine house to generate its own electricity at the rear. A plain, almost church-like frontage included a single high window in the operators' room; there was a glass canopy stretching across the whole width, beneath which were two sets of doors and a bay-windowed pay box. A small entrance hall led, via heavy, red velvet curtains, into the auditorium, which accommodated 360 people. In front of the screen and curtains was a small pit complete with piano, and the operators' room was equipped with the latest Pathé projector.

Local resident Ralph Rumble, now a youthful ninety-year-old, recalled that the seating, on a sloping floor, was made up entirely of six-foot benches with hinged seats and no armrests. They were covered in black rexine stuffed with horsehair. Ralph's cinema-going days began in 1919 when, at the age of eight, he queued up on the gravel forecourt of the Peoples' Electric, along with a crowd of boys and girls, before paying their 1d admission to the Saturday afternoon matinée. In particular, he remembers the Pearl White serials, Fatty Arbuckle, Chester Conklin, the Keystone Cops and the Westerns of Tom Mix and 'Lightning' Brice. Musical accompaniment was provided by local pianist Ruby Letherby, while a retired policeman, Mr Diabold, acted as a bouncer.

THE PEOPLE'S ELECTRIC THEATRE,
STATION ROAD, YIEWSLEY.

The Management of the above Theatre beg to announce that it will be

OPENED on SATURDAY, JAN. 28th,

WHEN A

Strong Programme of Pictures

WILL BE PRESENTED, BOTH INSTRUCTIVE AND AMUSING.

Only the Best and most Up-to-date Pictures will be shown.

☛ *COME AND DECIDE FOR YOURSELF.* ☚

The Theatre is just outside the Station, thus affording every facility to those Patrons coming by Rail.

Matinee 3 o'clock.   Evening 6.30 to 10.30 continuous.

☛ *BIOYOLES STORED FREE.* ☚

Prices : 3d., 6d., and a few Reserved Seats 1s.

Local press announcement for the opening of Yiewsley's first cinema, the Peoples' Electric Theatre, in January 1911.

Ralph said that the ex-PC 'did his best to keep the kids quiet and make them sit down' – apparently quite a hard task. He also remarked that by 1920 the interior of the building had deteriorated; the seat coverings had been vandalized (even in those days); and the cinema's nickname 'the fleapit' was more than justified!

But back in 1911, great excitement had been engendered by the novelty of the town's first picture house, and it soon attracted large crowds. Performances were continuous from 6.30 p.m. to 10.30 p.m., in addition to the Saturday matinée. Admission prices were 3d and 6d, with a few reserved 1s seats at the back, which Ralph thought were usually booked by courting couples. What he actually said was 'the back row was occupied by those who had other ideas on their minds!'

It was reported that within a year of the cinema's opening, some people were paying five or six visits a week, which resulted in the management instigating a Wednesday matinée. Among a number of successful films shown was *The Fall of Troy*, and a newsreel scoop screened on 1 July 1911 was the filming of King George V's Coronation which had taken place only eight days earlier on 23 June.

But ten years on from the opening, events were conspiring to signal the end of the Peoples' Electric. First came an announcement in January 1921 that plans were underway

114

for a 'fine, new cinema' to be built at the other end of the High Street. Then, in October, the 1,000-seat Savoy opened in Uxbridge, easily reachable from Yiewsley on the $2\frac{1}{2}$-mile GWR branch line, in a journey time of seven minutes. Added to that was the run-down condition of the Peoples' Electric, so probably it was no surprise when the end came in 1922.

Four years later, it was converted into a motor repair workshop with two petrol pumps on the forecourt, and named Pat's Garage. But it was still recognizable as the old cinema, since the owner retained most of the original features, including the raked floor, projection room and pay box, together with their windows. It has since been demolished and the open space is used for a weekly market.

Incidentally, Ralph Rumble, who went into the building trade, was one of the army of workmen who helped to build the Uxbridge Regal in 1931. He told me that he worked a 77-hour week, from Sunday to Saturday, for an hourly wage of 1s 7d. He added that at the height of the Depression, he considered himself one of the more fortunate.

The plans for the new Yiewsley cinema, first announced early in 1921, did not come to fruition for another two and a half years. Final approval was not granted until February 1923, but the building was completed within seven months. Christened with the somewhat unusual name of the Marlborough, it occupied a commanding corner position at the junction of St Stephen's Road and the High Street. The main construction work was carried out by Hansom Contractors of Southall, while all interior decorations and ornamental stonework were entrusted to London-based craftsmen G. Jackson and Sons and P. Turpin. The total cost, including the two shops incorporated into the frontage, was £15,000. The main entrance was extremely small, but flanked as it was on both sides by average-sized shop fronts and set under a solid rectangular canopy, created the impression of a much wider façade. Two front steps led into a tiny foyer housing the manager's office and pay box, with two staircases up to the balcony. The auditorium decor was described by the local press as 'Neo-Grec', or as they explained 'the ancient Greek art adapted to modern requirements'. Both side walls were divided up by pilasters with finely modelled Grecian Ionic caps, bearing a cornice ornately decorated with a leaf pattern. The ceiling was described as 'flat, arched, panelled with a Guilloche band; and fitted with ventilation and light points, designed to form part of the decorative scheme'. In fact, the interior resembled a smaller version of the Uxbridge Savoy built two years earlier, with a narrow, rectangular auditorium, medium-sized circle, plain proscenium arch and a smallish stage. But overall, the Marlborough was considerably smaller, seating only 408 in the stalls and 146 in the balcony.

The cinema had been constructed under the supervision of the general manager W.M. Euerby, and was formally opened by the chairman of Yiewsley council, F.E. Dominey JP, on Monday 24 September 1923. The opening programme consisted of a Jackie Coogan picture *Circus Days*, supported by several 'two-reelers' and an edition of *Pathé Gazette*, all accompanied by a full orchestra. Films shown at the Marlborough were always several weeks old; programmes changed on Mondays and Thursdays; admission charges were 5d, 9d, 1s 3d, 1s 6d and 1s 10d. After a while stage acts were introduced – usually a double act and, it must be said, not 'headliners'.

After operating successfully for ten years, the cinema was enlarged to meet popular

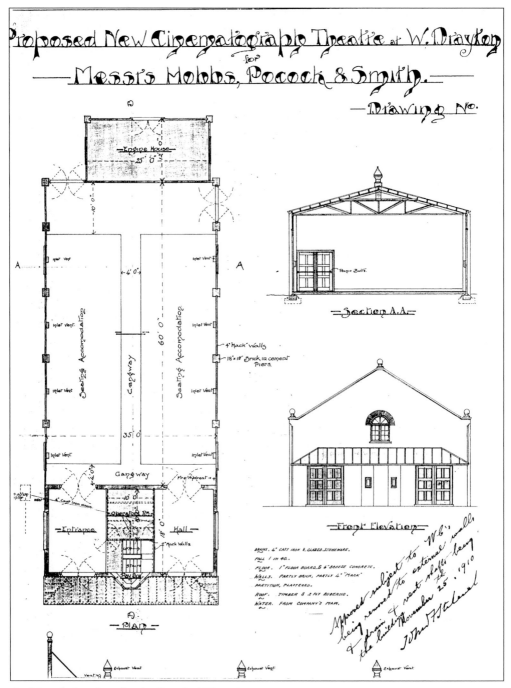

Architect's drawings for the Peoples' Electric.

demand and after refurbishment reopened on 15 September 1933, its seating capacity having been increased to 989. On 27 December, a special children's matinée performance of the pantomime *Puss in Boots* was presented, with every child receiving a Christmas present. The Marlborough remained under the same management until the mid-thirties. The enterprising Mr Euerby had always splashed out on his newspaper advertising. Invariably, his weekly block advertisements were much grander and more prominently displayed than those of his bigger competitors. After the advent of sound films, he introduced Wednesday and Saturday matinées, and the cinema continued to play to packed houses.

But then along with the Regal and Savoy in Uxbridge, the Marlborough was swallowed up by Union Cinemas until the end of 1937, when all three houses became part of the ABC circuit's take-over. Throughout the war and post-war years, the cinema continued to serve the local community (at least those people who were prepared to wait a while for new films to come round, rather than make the short trip to Uxbridge or elsewhere). For others, it provided an opportunity to catch up on the pictures they had missed.

By 1956, like so many others, the cinema had started on the downward slide, resulting in a brief shutdown before reopening in August under the new ownership of Loris Cinemas, and with a new name, the Ritz. It had again been refurbished and installed with Cinemascope, enabling *The Robe* to be shown at the reopening. The children's Saturday morning shows had been discontinued some time previously, but it was hoped that they would be revived in the near future.

However, after only sixteen months, with television having a devastating effect on audiences, it was reported that the Ritz was losing around £2,000 per year. The proprietors requested a three-year loan from the council, and when it was refused, made an appeal to local businessmen for financial aid. The appeal, which received strong support from an unexpected quarter, the local clergy – and in particular the Revd A.H. Woodhouse, vicar of St Martin's, West Drayton – eventually bore fruit, together with a consolation grant of £200 from the council.

Meanwhile the cinema had closed again for a short period. And again it made another comeback under yet another new owner. But this brought about a complete change of policy, resulting in the screening of a series of X-rated continental films. Ironically, the clergy were now obliged to do a U-turn and, along with many others, strongly condemned the programmes. Consequently, when the Ritz's licence came up for renewal in 1959, it was refused. And in April 1960 the cinema closed after showing two quite harmless and innocuous films, namely Priestley's *The Good Companions* and a B Western *Last of the Badmen*. Evidently the owners had got the message – but unfortunately too late.

The building was converted to a Mac Fisheries supermarket; then a Timberland DIY store, and was finally demolished in November 1983. I watched as the walls came tumbling down after a battering by the big ball and chain, which showed no respect for neo-Grecian art, as it reduced the red and green plaster cornices to rubble – a truly sorry sight! Eventually, an office block was erected on the site, which is currently occupied by Hillingdon Health Authority.

Newspaper advertisement for the opening of the Marlborough cinema, Yiewsley, in September 1923.

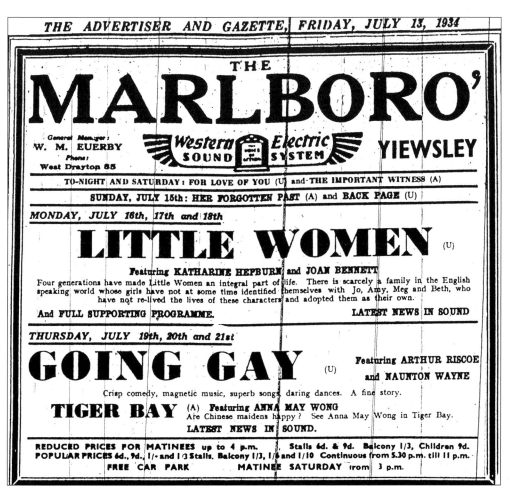

THE

MARLBORO'

General Manager:
W. M. EUERBY
Phone:
West Drayton 85

Western SOUND *Electric* SYSTEM

YIEWSLEY

TO-NIGHT AND SATURDAY: FOR LOVE OF YOU (U) and THE IMPORTANT WITNESS (A)

SUNDAY, JULY 15th: HER FORGOTTEN PAST (A) and BACK PAGE (U)

MONDAY, JULY 16th, 17th and 18th

LITTLE WOMEN (U)

Featuring **KATHARINE HEPBURN** and **JOAN BENNETT**

Four generations have made Little Women an integral part of life. There is scarcely a family in the English speaking world whose girls have not at some time identified themselves with Jo, Amy, Meg and Beth, who have not re-lived the lives of these characters and adopted them as their own.

And **FULL SUPPORTING PROGRAMME.**   **LATEST NEWS IN SOUND**

THURSDAY, JULY 19th, 20th and 21st

GOING GAY (U)

Featuring **ARTHUR RISCOE** and **NAUNTON WAYNE**

Crisp comedy, magnetic music, superb songs, daring dances. A fine story.

TIGER BAY (A) Featuring ANNA MAY WONG

Are Chinese maidens happy? See Anna May Wong in Tiger Bay.

LATEST NEWS IN SOUND.

REDUCED PRICES FOR MATINEES up to 4 p.m.   Stalls 6d. & 9d.   Balcony 1/3, Children 9d.
POPULAR PRICES 6d., 9d., 1/- and 1/3 Stalls. Balcony 1/3, 1/6 and 1/10 Continuous from 5.30 p.m. till 11 p.m.
FREE CAR PARK   **MATINEE SATURDAY from 3 p.m.**

A large local press advertisement for the Marlborough in 1934. Note that the same General Manager, Mr W.M. Euerby, had been in office since the opening in 1923.

119

The Marlborough, frontage in 1937, while still under the ownership of Union Cinemas, and before the take-over by ABC. At one time, tickets could be reserved at the tobacconist and confectioner's next door, the Marlborough Sweet Stores.

A view of the rather narrow auditorium of the Marlborough, as seen from the stage, showing the extremely small balcony.

The Marlborough auditorium viewed from the balcony, depicting the plain but pleasant décor.

The former Marlborough, now re-named the Ritz, pictured in the late 1950s, shortly before its closure.

Five
Iver: From Estate Hall to Furniture Warehouse

In 1928, a unique village cinema was built just over the West Drayton border, in the Richings Park area of Iver. Although it was outside the boundary demarcation of what is now the borough of Hillingdon, it was, nevertheless, patronised by the people from Yiewsley, West Drayton and Uxbridge, and in fact, went out of its way to entice them to this somewhat distant outpost.

Known during construction as the Richings Estate Hall and, when completed, as the Plaza, this was another example of a cinema built adjacent to a housing development, in this case the Richings Park estate. The same building firm, Gradwell's of Barrow-in-Furness, was involved, and the architect was George E. Clare. Mr Clare designed a mock Tudor-style exterior, giving the building the appearance of a large manor house. Measuring 125ft by 51ft, it housed seating accommodation for 580 all on one level, although a miniature balcony was provided solely for the Duke and Duchess of Kent, who lived nearby. It is not recorded whether they ever used it.

Described by the local press as 'palatial', the Plaza incorporated a roomy entrance hall with a café immediately above, looking out onto a veranda, a large stage, two dressing rooms, and an auditorium 77ft by 44ft. There were three blocks of tip-up seats, upholstered in powder blue velvet, set on a wood-block floor partially covered with Wilton carpeting. The cost of the building was £15,000 and a Compton organ was later installed for an additional £3,000. Built on a site adjoining Iver GWR station on the main line from Paddington, the cinema soon became a familiar landmark, with its name boldly displayed in red neon lighting. The Richings Park Estate (1928) Ltd appointed as the Plaza's first general manager K.A. Van Beine, who lived on the estate, and already managed a number of picture theatres. He was also in the music business, and formed an orchestra to play at the opening on Monday 6 August 1928. Their recital was followed by the silent film *The Leopard Lady* starring Jacqueline Logan.

The general policy was to change the programme on Mondays and Thursdays, but quite often the Plaza presented a special attraction which ran for the whole week, with matinées on Wednesday and Saturday. An example of this was *The Broadway Melody*, the first 'talkie' to be shown there in November 1929, while a year later, *Journey's End* was held over for a second week. Billed as a 'Gigantic Attraction', it was shown at the same time as the London release date, and screened four times a day. The more expensive seats (2s 4d and 3s 6d) could be booked in advance at the box office and at Willis's Music Shop in Uxbridge, while extra buses were run from two points in Uxbridge, in addition to the usual free service that the cinema provided from Yiewsley station at twenty minute intervals. Patrons were spoilt for choice, since the train journey took only three minutes! The Plaza's bus services were advertised in local newspapers under the headline 'Get a Real Good Bus Ride Free – To See a Real Good Show', and a timetable listing various pick-up points was also printed. The management frequently took out extremely large block advertisements for its programmes, but admission charges were slightly higher than average, with the 2s 4d and 3s 6d seats advertised as 'special fauteuils'.

The cinema underwent a change of ownership in 1930, when the proprietor

A 1934 picture of the Iver Plaza.

PLAZA THEATRE

IVER (Next to Iver G.W.R. Station) Bucks

GENERAL MANAGER ... ... K. A. VAN BIENE.

GRAND OPENING

MONDAY, AUGUST 6th, at 3 p.m.

———— DOORS OPEN 2.30. ————

THIS THEATRE WILL BE OPENED AS A HIGH-CLASS FAMILY CINEMA, SHOWING THE PICK OF THE WORLD'S PRODUCTIONS, AND MUSIC PROVIDED BY A SELECT LONDON ORCHESTRA.

CONTINUOUS PERFORMANCE DAILY FROM 6 p.m. TILL 10.45 p.m.
MATINEES SATURDAYS & BANK HOLIDAYS AT 3 p.m.

Popular Prices: 2/4, 1/10, 1/3 and 6d.

Watch this Space for Title of Enormous Opening Attraction

NOTICE.

On SATURDAY, August 4th, prior to the Theatre opening as a Cinema, the RICHINGS PLAYERS will present the "HAPPY ENDING," by Ian Hay, a play in three acts.

Special Prices for this night only: 5/9, 3/6, 2/4, 1/10 Reserved, and 1/3 Unreserved. Seats can be booked on and after July 28th, at the Richings Park Estate Office, where the plan can be seen.

Local press announcement for the opening of the Plaza, Iver, in August 1928.

was listed as Edwin G. Griffiths, and again in 1934 after a brief closure for redecoration. When it reopened on 14 May with *College Humour* starring Bing Crosby, the posters announced that it was 'under entirely new management'. Occasionally a stage production or orchestral concert was presented as an alternative to a picture show – and in fact the local dramatic society, the Richings Players, had been the first users of the Plaza when they staged the play *The Happy Ending* on 4 August 1928, prior to the official opening on 6 August.

But despite its early successes, its extensive advertising and free transport services, the Plaza found it difficult to compete during the rest of the decade. New luxury cinemas had been springing up in the surrounding areas, and its out-of-the-way location was a distinct disadvantage. When war came in 1939, the ownership had passed to Chiswick Productions Cinemas Ltd run by Mr G. Norrish, who decided that the building could be used more profitably for storing furniture. And in late October 1940, a notice appeared on the entrance doors that read: 'This Cinema Closed Through War Conditions'. An abrupt end to what had been a brief lifespan of only twelve years.

Mr Norrish appointed one of his employees, Mr Brum, and Mr Brum's wife as caretakers of the store, and they moved into the Plaza, using the dressing rooms as living quarters. Mrs Brum, now a West Drayton resident, told me how the auditorium was filled with furniture from floor to ceiling, while the ladies' cloakroom housed a collection of pianos that included a Bechstein grand. And when a sudden thaw followed the severe winter of 1946-7, both the Bechstein and Compton organ were ruined by the flooding – as were the organ chambers under the stage. She also told me about a mystery that was never solved. During the first years that she was in residence – in addition to the furniture deliveries – cans of film continued to arrive at regular intervals. Perhaps news of the Plaza's closure had not got around!

When it had outlived its usefulness as a furniture storage depot, the former cinema stood idle for a time, and then the bulldozers moved in. It was demolished in 1962, and replaced by an apartment block.

During my discussion with film historian William K. Everson, referred to earlier, he mentioned that in his many years of cinema-going in London and the outlying suburbs, he had never managed to visit the Plaza. He hoped that I could enlighten him about the missing link in his chain, but coincidentally, and to my regret, I too, had never seen the inside of the Iver cinema.

A September 1928 newspaper advertisement giving details of the Plaza's free bus services throughout the area.

PLAZA THEATRE
IVER General Manager : K. A. VAN BIENE. BUCKS

ENORMOUS ATTRACTION.

The Greatest "TALKIE" yet.

Week Commencing MONDAY, NOVEMBER 25th.

EVERY EVENING at 6 p.m. and 8.15 p.m.

THE

BROADWAY
MELODY

ALL TALKING.   ALL SINGING AND DANCING.

MATINEES—Wednesday & Saturday at 2.45 p.m.

NO ALTERATION IN PRICES OF ADMISSION

All the Very Best and Latest Talking Films will be Shown at this Theatre in Addition to Silent Pictures.

Bus or Train from West Drayton, and Buses direct from Uxbridge get you to our Theatre

The Plaza, Iver, proudly announces the showing of its first 'talkie' in November 1929.

Another example of the Plaza's large-scale newspaper advertising for its latest epic sound film in 1930.